Teaching Christianity

at Key Stage 1

Teaching Christianity

at Key Stage 1

Alison Seaman and Graham Owen

Illustrations by Ken Mckie

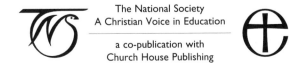

The National Society
A Christian Voice in Education

a co-publication with
Church House Publishing

The National Society/Church House Publishing
Church House
Great Smith Street
London SW1P 3NZ

ISBN 0 7151 4912 1

Published in 1999 by the National Society (Church of England) for Promoting Religious
Education and Church House Publishing

Cover design and icons by Leigh Hurlock

Printed in England by Cromwell Press Ltd, Trowbridge, Wiltshire

Contents

Introduction

Teaching children about Christianity has been described as being like treading on eggshells and avoiding thunderbolts. In a group of teachers we worked with recently, two of them expressed their fears about teaching Christianity. One was concerned because she was an atheist, the other because he was a Christian. Both were worried that they would influence, even indoctrinate, their impressionable young pupils with their own views. Sadly, these concerns led both of them to avoid teaching Christianity whenever possible. Our aim in this book is to provide a resource that will support those who feel uncertain about teaching Christianity as well as giving further food for thought to those who feel more confident but who would like some different ideas. In writing it we have tried to take account of the work we have done over the years with teachers working at Key Stage 1.

Through the themes chosen for this book we have provided a range of activities by which the children will be introduced to some key Christian beliefs and practices. There are also opportunities to think about, discuss and explore the different ideas. We have attempted to demonstrate some of the wealth of Christian traditions that make up this extremely diverse world faith. It would be impossible to represent every style and approach but we hope we have captured something of the diversity that can be found, not just in this country but around the world.

Some aspects of Christian belief and practice are flamboyant and visibly or audibly attractive. Some aspects are less obviously eye catching, but are of no less importance. There is always a temptation to present the more exotic or sensational examples. In our choice of themes we have tried to ensure that the underlying meaning and significance for Christians is always given consideration.

Getting started

You will find a wide range of Christian ideas have been introduced in each section of the book. These were chosen to reflect some of the most popular areas of study to be found in Agreed Syllabuses and Diocesan Syllabuses for Religious Education. Close reference has been made to the recommendations of the SCAA Working Group Report, which accompanies the Model Syllabuses for Religious Education and also to The National Society's booklet *Christianity in the Agreed Syllabus.*

In each section we have introduced a range of options that are easy to prepare and which engage the children in a variety of activities. These are mostly practical activities and involve 'doing' and 'making'. They are accompanied by 'thinking' activities that can be carried out in a group or individually. These provide an opportunity for reflection and personal response. They could also act as a focus for collective worship.

Each chapter of the book follows a similar pattern and is addressed to the teacher. The sections have been written in response to the questions we are asked most frequently about teaching Christianity. For example:

I've got to teach about Christianity and I don't know anything about it. What do I need to know?

It will help to know that . . . will provide you with background information to enable you build upon and develop your own subject knowledge.

I don't really know what it is about Christianity I'm supposed to be teaching. What should I teach?

Key ideas . . . will help you to identify the Christian ideas that lie behind the activities. Remember that at Key Stage 1 you are putting the building blocks in place for the future. The key ideas help you to see what the children are working towards.

I don't know one end of a Bible from the other. Can you help?

The Bible can help you . . . gives Bible references to which you can refer if you want to explore the themes for yourself. Don't worry, you will soon find your way around it!

I've run out of ideas for things to do and there's so little time to prepare. What can I do?

Start by . . . , Then . . . , Follow this by . . . Most sections of the book contain three activities and these are intended to stand alone. Each activity is broken down into a series of stages. We have tried to minimize your preparation time by providing as much information as possible. We have, for example, given brief outlines of stories to enable you to retell them in your own words, ensuring you cover the key points. We have also given suggested wording to help you to introduce to the children some of the more complex Christian concepts. The activities are intended to be as straightforward as possible while using a variety of teaching styles and approaches.

The activities could be completed as a set or you could revisit the theme once a term or once a year, completing one activity each time. There is also flexibility in the way the themes could be used and linked together. The material could be integrated with work about other world faiths. For example, the section called 'The Bible' could form part of a study of holy books, or the section on 'Light' could be developed to include a study of the significance of light in other world faiths.

What about the children's spiritual development?

The whole process of working with these activities will contribute to children's spiritual development. The pupils are encouraged to raise questions, to engage with the Christian ideas and explore these ideas through creative and reflective activities. Be adventurous and have fun!

How do I answer the children's 'difficult' questions?

Questions like 'Who is God?' and 'What does God look like?' or 'How did the world begin?' or even 'Why did my pet rabbit die?' are the sort of questions that all of us think about at some point in our lives – and children are no exception. Don't worry if you feel inadequate in responding to these universal mysteries, we all do! It might help to see your work with the children as an opportunity to take part in a quest towards finding meaning and purpose in our lives. The whole education process makes a contribution to this. We are all in our own way grappling with mystery and by giving the children the opportunity to explore their ideas, we are helping them to develop the skills, the language and the confidence to join us in that quest.

One of the most helpful strategies is to try to approach teaching Christianity in the same way as other curriculum areas. This may well require stepping back or detaching ourselves from the material we teach. Looking at the language we use can help us with this. For example, when talking about religious beliefs and practices, of whatever religion, it is more appropriate to adopt the position of observer; rather than talking about 'our beliefs' or 'our prayers' we could say 'this is what Christians believe' or 'this is a prayer that Christians say'. Throughout the book we have tried to provide examples of how you might do this when introducing Christian ideas to your class.

Finally, a word about religion in general, which can, and often does, get a 'bad press'. The cultural and historical significance of Christianity is sometimes portrayed as merely a historical phenomenon and something not relevant in the contemporary world. This is an opportunity to introduce children to a living faith that is a significant force in the lives of many people throughout the world today.

# The Bible

It will help to know that . . .

The Bible is the most important book for Christians and is central to Christian belief. It has been translated into more languages than any other book in the world – in fact, more than 2,000 different languages. In churches throughout the world the Bible is used in worship, for teaching and for study. Many Christians possess a Bible of their own and regularly set aside time to read it.

The Bible is not just one book but a large collection of books written over a long period of time by many different authors. The collection is divided into two main sections. Christians call the first collection the Old Testament. These books were first written in Hebrew and tell the story of the Jewish people. These are the Scriptures that Jesus knew and on which he based his teaching.

The books of the New Testament were also written by different authors during the 1st century AD. It is quite different from the Hebrew Bible. It has four accounts of the life of Jesus, called the Gospels, and a collection of books and letters recounting the experience of the early church. Translating and interpreting ancient texts is an ongoing process. This activity was greatly enhanced by the discovery of a series of ancient scrolls and fragments near the Dead Sea in 1947.

Rather than reading the Bible from cover to cover, Christians generally use the book in different ways to discover its meaning for their lives today. Interpretations vary considerably and range from accepting the Bible as literally true at all times to considering the Bible as texts to be interpreted in the light of one's own Christian experience.

Key ideas . . .

- ◆ The Bible is the sacred book for Christians.
- ◆ It was written a long time ago, but is still used by Christians today.
- ◆ It is made up of a collection of many books.

The Bible can help you . . .

For this unit there are no specific Bible references, but you may find it helpful to use a full version of the Bible (rather than a children's abridged version) to show the book in its entirety.

Key words . . .

Bible, books, Old Testament, New Testament

ACTIVITY 1 A SPECIAL BOOK FOR CHRISTIANS

You will need . . .

Bibles of different sizes and styles and with different bindings, electronic versions of the Bible, e.g. diskette, CD ROM, etc.

Start by . . .

. . . asking the children to choose their favourite book – some may want to bring a book from home – which might be a favourite story book or may be a religious one. After sharing these with the class, make a display of them. Ask the children to explain . . .

My favourite book is special to me because . . .

Ask the children if they keep their favourite book in a special place (if a child chooses a religious book she/he may be able to explain how it should be cared for and the way in which it is used by the family). Ask the children if the book is read often.

Then . . .

. . . visit a local church or chapel to discover where the Bible is kept and displayed. If a visit is not possible, use images to show this. You will notice that churches keep their Bibles in different ways, e.g. on a lectern, in the pews or in the pulpit.

Follow this by . . .

. . . explaining that the Bible is a special book for Christians.

It would be helpful to have a variety of different Bibles to explore. Draw attention to the different styles of presentation of the same book (remember you can purchase the Bible as a CD ROM). Add the Bibles to your display of special books.

It is important to emphasize that because it is a special book for Christians the Bible should be handled respectfully.

Something to think about . . .

Why do Christians try to read the Bible regularly?

The first Bibles were written out by hand. Think how long this must have taken!

ACTIVITY 2 MY STORY, OUR STORY

You will need . . .

. . . a Bible (to illustrate to the children that it is a collection of books), book making materials.

Start by . . .

. . . asking the children to share their own stories by saying which people are important to them, what their favourite places are and what activities they like to do.

Then . . .

. . . record their stories by using different literary styles, e.g. poetry, letters or stories. Encourage the children to devise titles for their books, e.g. *The Book of David, Nicola's Story, The Life of Rashid*, etc.

Follow this by . . .

. . . showing the children that the Bible contains the stories of the lives of many people and the events in their lives.

Make a collection of the children's stories into a class book. Show the children how the book tells the stories of the whole class and is a collection of stories, rather like the Bible.

Something to think about . . .

What kinds of stories do you like to read?

Who is your favourite author?

ACTIVITY 3 FINDING THE DEAD SEA SCROLLS

You will need . . .

. . . a small cardboard tube, e.g. an empty toilet roll, modelling clay, paint, paper.

Start by . . .

. . . telling the story of the shepherd boy who was looking after his sheep in the hills near the Dead Sea. He found some old pottery jars containing fragments of very ancient manuscripts. Thanks to his amazing discovery it has been possible to understand more about the Bible.

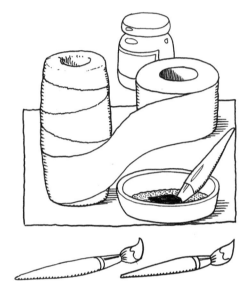

Make a replica of the Dead Sea Scrolls. Seal one end of a cardboard tube, and cover it with Medroc to make it into a container, with a small opening at the top. When it is dry, paint it a terracotta colour to make it look like an earthenware jar.

Then . . .

. . . 'distress' some paper to make it look like parchment by dabbing a damp tea bag over its surface. Under careful supervision, the edges could be singed to give it a very old appearance.

Follow this by . . .

. . . writing on it a verse from the Old Testament, for example:

> *Israel, remember this! The Lord – and the Lord alone – is our God.*

> *Love the Lord our God with all your heart, with all your soul, and with all your strength.*

Roll the parchment and slide it into the 'jar'.

Something to think about . . .

What books would you want children to read in 2000 years' time?

Will we still have books in the future?

The Old Testament

It will help to know that . . .

The Old Testament is one of the great classics of literature. It is a rich literary treasure of the ancient people of Israel. It was completed over a long period of time – it was begun in the Stone Age and was completed about the time that Jesus was born, about 2000 years ago.

Most of the book was originally written in Hebrew and has been translated into many different languages over the centuries, a process which still continues today.

The Old Testament is quite different in character from the New Testament in that there are very few books within it that can be positively identified to a particular author or date. Essentially, it is an anthology – a collection of writings by different authors from different ages.

The earliest editions of the Old Testament material were gathered together during the reigns of David and Solomon, at a time when Israel was becoming a prosperous nation, and the people of Israel were taking a keen interest in their history and their rise to fame and fortune. This was added to by the writings of the prophets, and many of these books contain their sermons and speeches dealing with various aspects of their national life.

The Old Testament also describes the period when the Hebrew nation was destroyed and the people led into slavery in Babylon. This had been predicted by many of the prophets. On their release from bondage Israel's leaders started to rebuild their nation and collect together the whole of Israel's national literature and to add their own contributions as well.

This section introduces children to three great stories from the Old Testament. While the meaning of these stories is multi-layered, the focus of each activity highlights key ideas within these stories.

Key ideas . . .

◆ The Old Testament (also called the Hebrew Bible) is the religious history of the Jewish people and their search for an understanding of God.

◆ It is a library of books written over a long period, a long time ago, by many different people.

◆ It contains different styles of literature, including stories, history and poetry.

The Bible can help you . . .

The birth of Moses can be found in Exodus 2.1-10. The story of Ruth is in the Book of Ruth, and the story of Jonah is in the Book of Jonah.

Key words . . .

Hebrew, Israel, history, prophet

ACTIVITY 1 THE STORY OF MOSES

You will need . . .

. . . the lid of a polystyrene egg box, a traditional wooden clothes peg (or miniature doll), scraps of fabric for clothing and bedding.

Start by . . .

. . . familiarizing yourself with the story of the birth of Moses. The key events in the story are:

◆ The Israelites were oppressed by their Egyptian rulers.

◆ All the boy babies were to be destroyed by drowning them in the River Nile.

◆ Moses' mother hid him in the bullrushes to save him from this fate.

◆ He was discovered by Pharaoh's daughter, who took pity on him.

◆ She employed a woman to look after him and bring him up.

◆ It had been arranged that this woman was actually Moses' mother.

◆ Moses' life had been saved.

Then . . .

. . . make a Moses basket, using the top of the egg box, and pad the basket with material. Make your clothes peg into a baby Moses, by swaddling it with the scraps of material and drawing a face on the top of the clothes peg. Put the baby into the basket and float it on a bowl of water.

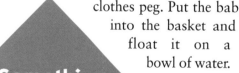

Something to think about . . .

Imagine the excitement when a new baby is born.

Pharaoh's daughter rescued Moses and was very kind to him. Who will you be kind to today?

Follow this by . . .

. . . telling the children that when Moses grew up, he became a great leader and helped the Israelites to escape from slavery in Egypt.

Try learning the song 'When Israel was in Egypt's land, let my people go!' (*Junior Praise*, number 276 (Burt, Horrobin and Leavers), see Resources list).

ACTIVITY 2 THE STORY OF RUTH

You will need . . .

. . . simple book making equipment, e.g. folded card for a zigzag book.

Start by . . .

. . . telling the story of Ruth (one of the shortest books in the Bible). You could retell the story in your own words based on this outline:

◆ Naomi and her daughter-in-law Ruth were very sad because their husbands had died.

◆ Naomi decided she was going back to Bethlehem, her home town.

◆ Ruth said she would go with her.

◆ They set out on their long journey home.

◆ Ruth worked hard in the fields, which were owned by Boaz.

◆ Ruth got married to Boaz.

◆ Later Ruth had a baby called Obed.

◆ Naomi was very happy and enjoyed looking after her grandson.

Then . . .

. . . explore how Naomi felt:

◆ when she thought she was going away on her own;

◆ to have Ruth as a friend.

Follow this by . . .

. . . making a book of the story of Ruth. You could use the story outline as a guide.

Use this opportunity to explore with the children:

◆ what it is to be a good friend;

◆ the joys and challenges of being a loyal friend.

Something to think about . . .

How do you help your friends when they need you?

Which friend would you ask for help if you were in trouble?

ACTIVITY 3 THE STORY OF JONAH

You will need . . .

. . . card, scissors, colouring pencils, thin garden canes

Start by . . .

. . . telling the children the story of Jonah and the whale (Book of Jonah chapters 1 and 2). You could base your story on this outline:

- ◆ The people in the city of Nineveh were behaving very badly.

- ◆ God decided to send Jonah to make them change their ways.

- ◆ Jonah did not want to go and so tried to get away on board a ship sailing for Spain.

- ◆ A storm blew up and the crew blamed it on Jonah.

- ◆ The crew threw Jonah overboard.

- ◆ A whale saved Jonah and landed him near to the city of Nineveh.

- ◆ Jonah told the people of Nineveh to change their ways.

- ◆ God forgave them.

Then . . .

. . . discuss with the children how Jonah must have felt:

- ◆ when God asked him to go to Nineveh;

- ◆ as he was thrown overboard;

- ◆ when he was safe inside the whale.

Follow this by . . .

. . . making a moving model of Jonah and the whale (see illustration). Fix Jonah to the back of the whale so that he slides in and out of its mouth!

Something to think about . . .

Think about the things you are told to do, but that you do not want to do!

Jonah felt safe inside the whale . . . Where do you feel safe?

Jesus of Nazareth

It will help to know that . . .

. . . it could be argued that Jesus of Nazareth has affected the course of history more than any other individual who has ever lived. He is generally recognized as a great teacher and leader whose influence has been felt throughout the world. By Christians, however, he is acknowledged as Christ, a word that signifies their belief that he is the Son of God.

References other than those found in the Bible provide evidence of the existence of Jesus. He lived around 2,000 years ago in the country we now called Israel. Accounts of his life are to be found in the part of the Bible known as the New Testament. The four Gospels recall different events in Jesus' life, his teachings and the impact of these on the community in which he lived.

Little is known about his appearance. As a Jew, living in the Middle East, he probably looked like a Palestinian Arab. Artists throughout history and world-wide have depicted him within their own cultural setting or in a way which represents their belief about him. What is important, however, for Christians, is the man himself. His experience of humanity is both a comfort and an inspiration to them.

In this section, the activities are designed to introduce Jesus as a man, and the historical setting and geographical location of his life. There is a story from his early life with his family, and an event from his adult life which illustrates the way in which Jesus' actions challenged the norms of the society in which he lived.

Key ideas . . .

◆ Jesus is the central figure for Christians.

◆ Although Jesus lived a long time ago, he is still important for Christians today.

◆ The actions and ideas of Jesus changed the lives of many of his contemporaries, and continue to influence the lives of people today.

The Bible can help you . . .

Mention is made of Jesus' early life in Luke 2.39-40 and 51-52. The story 'Lost in Jerusalem' can be found in Luke 2.41-52 and 'Jesus visits Zacchaeus' in Luke 19.1-9.

Key words . . .

Jew, Nazareth, New Testament, Gospel

ACTIVITY 1 JESUS AT HOME

You will need . . .

. . . cardboard packets and small boxes, paint, scissors, modelling material, picture references to illustrate the historical setting.

Start by . . .

. . . describing some of the things that are known about Jesus of Nazareth. You could use some of these ideas to set the scene.

◆ Jesus lived around 2000 years ago.

◆ He lived with his family in a town called Nazareth in the country we now call Israel.

◆ His mother was called Mary and his father Joseph. He had brothers and sisters.

◆ Joseph, his father, was a carpenter and Jesus would probably have helped his father, learning how to make and build things with wood and stone.

Then . . .

. . . make models of houses like the one in which Jesus would have lived.

Using the modelling materials, make some of the things that Jesus' family would have used:

◆ jugs to carry water;

◆ food pots and bowls;

◆ oil lamps;

◆ mats and mattresses;

Encourage the children to think about the ways in which Jesus' home would have been different from their homes. For example, there would have been no electricity, no cars and no computers.

Follow this by . . .

. . . using the children's models to explore a day with Jesus' family in Nazareth. For example

◆ going to the well for water;

◆ helping in the carpenter's workshop;

◆ following the sheep as the shepherd drives them through the town;

◆ lighting the oil lamps at night;

◆ sleeping on the roof in the warm weather.

Something to think about . . .

What must it have been like to live without electricity, cars or televisions?

What is the best thing about my home?

ACTIVITY 2 LOST IN JERUSALEM

Start by . . .

. . . asking the children to describe times when they have been lost, for example being separated from their mum or dad in a supermarket.

Then . . .

. . . tell the story of when Jesus became separated from his family when he was a boy of twelve. You could use the outline below to retell the story. Try to encourage the children to identify with the characters in the story by stopping the story at the 'think spots'.

◆ Jesus and his family travelled to Jerusalem every year for the Passover festival. After the festival, his parents began the long journey home and were well on the way when they realized Jesus was not with them.

THINK SPOT

How did Joseph and Mary feel when they realized Jesus was not with them?

What do you think they did?

◆ When they could not find Jesus the family had to go all the way back. After searching and searching they eventually found Jesus in the temple sitting and talking with the temple's teachers (rabbis).

THINK SPOT

How do you think Joseph and Mary felt when they found Jesus?

What do you think they said to him?

◆ The temple teachers said Jesus was a very good pupil. Even though he was only twelve years old they were amazed by all the different questions he was asking them. Jesus was surprised that his mother and father did not know where to find him. He thought they would know he would be in the temple.

THINK SPOT

What do you think Mary and Joseph would have said to Jesus on the way home from Jerusalem?

Something to think about . . .

What things do I do that make my mum/dad/teacher happy?

What do I do that makes them sad or angry?

ACTIVITY 3 JESUS VISITS ZACCHAEUS

You will need . . .

. . . old newspapers, scissors, glue, stiff paper or thin card, scraps of material, crayons.

Start by . . .

. . . telling the story of Zacchaeus. You could follow the story outline below.

◆ Zacchaeus was a very rich tax collector. In those days tax collectors often took more than they should and kept the extra for themselves. He was very unpopular and nobody wanted to be his friend.

◆ Zacchaeus heard that Jesus was passing by and he wanted to see him.

◆ The crowds were so deep he could not see anything and so he climbed up into a tree for a better view.

◆ As Jesus walked past he called up to Zacchaeus and asked if he could stay at his home.

◆ Zacchaeus could not believe it. He came rushing down the tree and took Jesus to his home.

◆ The people in the crowd grumbled. They could not understand why Jesus wanted to be with Zacchaeus and not with them.

◆ Zacchaeus told Jesus he was sorry for being greedy, and for all the wrong things he had done.

◆ He said he would pay back all the people he had cheated.

Something to think about . . .

Have you ever been in a crowd of people waiting to see something or somebody? What did it feel like? Were you able to see anything?

If you could invite a famous person home for tea, who would it be? What would you talk to that person about?

Then . . .

. . . act out the story. As it unfolds, encourage the children to identify with the feelings of Zacchaeus and the people in the crowds. Explore together why Jesus took his friends and followers by surprise when he chose to go to the home of Zacchaeus.

Follow this by . . .

. . . making models of Zacchaeus in the tree. Roll newspaper into a tube and secure it with tape. Fringe one end to make the tree. Gently pull out the cut ends from the centre of the tube, while holding the base securely. Cut out a face on a long tab of card and colour it with the crayons. Use scraps of fabric to make a head covering. Push the tab down into the fringed end of the newspaper so the face appears at the top.

More about Jesus

It will help to know that . . .

It is clear from the Gospel accounts and from other early writings that Jesus' life had a considerable impact upon the people with whom he lived and worked. As an adult he became famous as a preacher, teacher and healer. He was renowned for his care of the sick, for people in need and for the marginalized in his community. He was also someone who challenged the accepted norms of society. He inspired great commitment from many of his followers but he also made enemies.

During his ministry, Jesus drew large crowds to hear him speak. He often used parables (stories about daily lives with a deeper meaning) which helped his followers to understand more about God. There can be no doubt that he also did some remarkable things, described by Christians as miracles or 'mighty works'. Throughout the centuries people have pondered on these events and the many possible explanations. For some Christians, the miracles are accepted literally, while others try to discover a rational meaning. Whichever argument is followed, what is significant is that Christians believe that in his life and actions Jesus demonstrated in visible and practical ways that God's creative power is at work in the world.

Key ideas . . .

◆   Jesus made a notable impact upon the people he met.

◆   The Bible records that Jesus taught his followers about God, healed the sick and performed miracles.

The Bible can help you . . .

◆   The story of how Jesus restored sight is found in Mark 10.46-52, in Matthew 20.29-34 and in Luke 18.35-43.

◆   The parable Jesus told about the lost sheep is found in Matthew 18.10-14 and in Luke 15.3-7.

◆   The story of how Jesus fed five thousand people is found in all the Gospels: Matthew 14.13-21, Mark 6.30-44, Luke 9.10-17 and John 6.1-14.

Key words . . .

teacher, healer, parable, miracle

ACTIVITY 1 HEALING BARTIMAEUS

You will need . . .

. . . blindfolds.

Start by . . .

. . . finding some volunteers who are willing to be blindfolded. Ask the children to try to complete some simple tasks while blindfolded, for example, to find the classroom door, to complete a simple jigsaw puzzle or to string some beads.

Then . . .

. . . ask them to describe how it feels to try these tasks without being able to see. Do their other senses help them with these tasks?

Follow this by . . .

. . . introducing the story of Bartimaeus. You could use this story outline.

◆ Bartimaeus was blind. He wanted to meet Jesus, because he believed that Jesus could help him.

◆ He could not see Jesus so he called out his name and asked for his help.

◆ Jesus heard him calling and asked for Bartimaeus to be brought to him.

◆ Jesus knew Bartimaeus trusted him and Bartimaeus was healed.

◆ Everyone was amazed by what had happened.

Something to think about . . .

What do you enjoy using your eyes to look at?

Could your school support a national organization that helps blind people?

ACTIVITY 2 THE LOST SHEEP

You will need . . .

. . . circles of card (about the size of a saucer), strips of white, black and brown paper (about 10 cm long), scissors, glue, colouring pencils.

Start by . . .

. . . asking the children if they have ever lost something precious to them. Explore this situation together.

Then . . .

. . . retell Jesus' story about the shepherd who lost one of his sheep. Explore the shepherd's feelings when he:

◆ realized one of his sheep was missing;

◆ had to search for it;

◆ finally found the lost sheep.

Explain that when Jesus told this story he was trying to help people to understand more about what God is like. Jesus wanted his followers to know that God loves and cares for everybody, especially if they feel lost and unhappy.

Follow this by . . .

. . . making sheep.

◆ Draw the sheep's face in the middle of the circle of card.

◆ Add the fleece by curling the strips of white, brown and black paper and sticking them around the face.

◆ Use the sheep for a wall display or hang them as mobiles.

◆ The children's responses to the story could be included in your display.

Something to think about . . .

Who is there to help me when I feel lost?

When can I help someone who feels lost?

ACTIVITY 3 JESUS SHARES A MEAL

You will need . . .

. . . one soft bread roll.

Start by . . .

. . . saying that you would like to give everyone a bread roll, but you only have one. Ask the children if they have any solutions to your problem.

Then . . .

. . . break up the roll until you have enough pieces so that everyone in the group can have some. It usually causes some amazement that one roll can be shared between a whole class, even though it is just a taste. Try to arrange that there is even some left over at the end.

Follow this by . . .

. . . explaining that the Bible describes a time when Jesus was faced with a similar problem. You could use this story outline.

- Jesus was so popular, large crowds used to follow him around.

- It was the end of a long day and people were hungry.

- There was not very much food – in the Bible it says a few loaves and some fishes.

- Jesus asked his friends to help him to share the food with everyone.

- Miraculously, there was enough for everyone to eat.

Something to think about . . .

What are your favourite meals?

Who would you share your favourite sweets with?

Advent, Christmas and Epiphany

It will help to know that . . .

Christmas is probably the best known Christian festival and has become part of the cultural and social fabric of society in many parts of the world.

The following range of activities explores the religious significance of Christmas for Christians. There are many rituals and customs associated with this season in the Christian calendar, which is sometimes described as the Christmas cycle. The traditional Christmas story is actually a compilation of two different narratives, one recorded by Matthew and the other by Luke.

Advent

The four weeks before Christmas is the season of Advent. This marks the beginning of the Christian year and is a time of preparation. For many, this time of the year is associated with rushing about buying presents, cooking and preparing extra food for the Christmas festivities. For Christians, however, there is a spiritual 'getting ready for Christmas', when time is taken to reflect on the coming of Jesus into the world. This reflective mood of Advent is visibly represented in some churches by the use of purple to cover the altar and for priestly vestments during worship in this season.

Key ideas about Advent . . .

- ◆ Advent is the beginning of the Christian year.
- ◆ Advent is a time when Christians look forward to and think about the birth of Jesus.
- ◆ Christians believe it is important to prepare themselves for special festivals.

The Bible can help you . . .

The Book of Isaiah in the Old Testament contains several well-known passages which Christians interpret as foretelling the birth of Jesus. These are Isaiah 7.10-16, Isaiah 9.2-7 and Isaiah 11.1-10. In the New Testament, in Matthew's Gospel 1.18-25 (especially verses 22 and 23) there is a reading about Mary, the mother of Jesus, fulfilling these prophecies.

Key words . . .

getting ready, waiting

Christmas

The coming of Jesus into the world forms the heart of the Christmas festival for Christians. This significant event has been described in several ways, for example, the birth of God's Son; a precious gift given by God to the whole world; a light shining into a dark world. Its particular significance for Christians is the belief that in Jesus, God became human, and experienced the joy and sadness of life. This central Christian belief (incarnation) is a distinctive feature of Christianity. When Christians read the Hebrew Scriptures they believe the coming of God into the world as Jesus was foretold; that Jesus was the Messiah prophesied by previous generations.

Key ideas about Christmas . . .

- ◆ At Christmas, Christians celebrate the birth of Jesus.
- ◆ Christians believe that Jesus is God's son.
- ◆ The story of Jesus' birth is told in the Bible.

The Bible can help you . . .

Both the Gospels of Luke (1.26–2.7) and Matthew (1.18-25) record the birth of Jesus. Angels bring news of the birth of Jesus to shepherds in Luke 2.8-20.

Key words . . .

birth, gift, light, Messiah

ACTIVITY 4   CHRISTMAS GIFTS

You will need . . .

. . . a piece of thin card approximately 15 cm square, Christmas wrapping paper, a cardboard box, e.g. a shoe box with a detachable lid, decorated to look like a Christmas gift.

Start by . . .

. . . discussing with the children some of the events around the birth of a new baby. Many of the children will have experience of this from their own family or close friends. Describe the custom of taking a gift to newly born babies, for example some clothing, a toy or some jewellery. You could make connections with the Christmas story in which traditional storytelling describes the shepherds bringing a lamb for the new-born baby.

Then . . .

. . . ask the children to think of a gift they would give to a special baby. Encourage them to think of something that is precious to them but not necessarily of great monetary value. Remember that the shepherds had few possessions and gave Jesus the only thing they owned.

Follow this by . . .

. . . asking the children to draw and/or write the name of their gift on one side of the piece of card. (They could also write their name if they want to.) The children may decorate the other side of the card with Christmas paper. The activity is concluded by sharing together as a group or class the gifts the children have chosen. Sit the children in a circle with the large decorated box in the middle. The children come forward and place their gifts in the box saying, 'My gift for the baby is . . .'

Something to think about . . .

What are the special occasions when you like to give gifts to your friends and family?

ACTIVITY 5 GIFTS FOR A KING

You will need . . .

. . . a collection of gold coloured objects (the children could contribute), oil of frankincense and myrrh (these can be obtained from shops that sell aromatherapy oils), aromatherapy oil burners.

Frankincense and myrrh can also be purchased in granular form to be burned over charcoal. Your local church may also be able to demonstrate this for you.

Start by . . .

. . . telling the story of the Magi visiting the baby Jesus. Different translations of the Bible use different forms to describe these visitors from the East, e.g. Magi, kings or astrologers. It is probable that they were scholars with a particular interest in astrology. Discuss the three gifts that the Magi gave to Jesus. They were not ordinary everyday things, but precious and exotic items. Your collection of gold coloured objects can be a starting point for the discussion.

Then . . .

. . . use the oil burners to discover the aroma of frankincense and myrrh. Explain that frankincense was used from the earliest times for worship. When it is burned the rising smoke reminds people that their prayers are being taken to God.

Myrrh is associated with death because it was used for anointing the dead and so pointed to the fact that Jesus would later die, and that his death would be very important to his followers. At Key Stage 1 the children need to understand the distinctive nature of these gifts. These were special gifts for a special baby.

Follow this by . . .

. . . asking the children to describe the aromas in their own words.

Something
to think about . . .

What is your favourite smell?

What does it make you think of?

*What is your most precious
possession?*

ACTIVITY 6 FOLLOW THE STAR

You will need . . .

. . . a nativity set (including a stable, Mary, Joseph and Jesus) and paper stars.

Start by . . .

. . . asking the children to describe a journey they have made – it could be a short journey, e.g. going to the shops or to a friend's house, or it could be a longer journey, e.g. going on holiday. Discuss the longer journeys the children have made. How did they travel? How did they find the way? What did they take with them on their journey?

Introduce the story of the Magi, who had to travel a long distance to find Jesus. Their guide for the journey was not a map but a bright shining star.

Then . . .

. . . make stars and write these words on them:

Follow this star to find Jesus

Set up a nativity scene (or use a picture) in a prominent place in your school. If you do not own a nativity set these can be made by the children. A stable, Mary, Joseph and Jesus are essential. You could add models of the shepherds, the wise men and animals that would have been found in the stable.

Something to think about . . .

Remember the time you made a long journey. How did you feel before setting off?

How did you feel when you arrived?

What did you do on your journey to pass the time away?

Follow this by . . .

. . . making a trail from the classroom to the place where you have set up your nativity scene. Use the stars to set the trail. You could take the children along the trail singing one of their favourite Christmas songs. On arrival at the Christmas crib you could sing 'Away in a Manger'.

Here comes spring!

It will help to know that . . .

Lent is an old English word for the season of spring. In the Christian calendar it marks the 40 days leading up to Easter. It commemorates the forty days and nights that Jesus spent alone, in the desert, when he fasted and contemplated his future ministry.

For Christians, Lent is a time of fasting and abstinence, reflection and repentance. In many churches, the colour purple is used for vestments to reflect the sombre nature of the season. Some Christians fast during this period and this traditionally meant giving up meat and rich foods. Many Christians today try to give up a favourite food or drink for Lent. More important is that Lent is a period of taking stock of life. It is a time for confession and seeking forgiveness. Christians might also undertake a period of study, attend more church services and seek ways of giving, both of their time and money, to charitable causes.

In some Western countries the custom has developed of spring cleaning homes during Lent. This external action reflects the inner process of thinking things through and sorting things out. Historically, rich foods were used up on Shrove Tuesday, the day before the Lent fast begins. This is the origin of the custom of eating pancakes. In some parts of the world this time is also known as Mardi Gras or Fat Tuesday and there are often elaborate street parades and carnivals.

Lent begins with the Christian festival called Ash Wednesday. In some traditions, palm crosses are burnt and the ash is used to make the sign of the cross on the forehead of worshippers. This ashing ceremony is a symbol of forgiveness and a reminder of human mortality.

Roughly half way through Lent there is a break from the austerity of the season, with the festival of Mothering Sunday.

Key ideas . . .

- Lent is the time leading up to Easter when Christians seek forgiveness for their sins.
- Shrove Tuesday, Ash Wednesday and Mothering Sunday are special days in the Christian calendar associated with Lent.

The Bible can help you . . .

Jesus' time of fasting in the desert is described in Matthew 4.1-2, Mark 1.12-13 and Luke 4.1-2.

Key words . . .

Lent, fasting, saying sorry, forgiveness, taking stock

ACTIVITY 1 SHROVE TUESDAY – CARNIVAL TIME

You will need . . .

. . . paper plates, collage materials, coloured paper streamers.

Start by . . .

. . . explaining that Shrove Tuesday is the day before the beginning of Lent. Christians fast during Lent, so the tradition arose of using up all the rich foods like fat and eggs by making pancakes. In some parts of the world Shrove Tuesday is celebrated with a carnival.

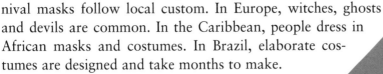

Then . . .

. . . make carnival masks by adding collage materials and coloured streamers to the paper plates. In different parts of the world traditions for styles of carnival masks follow local custom. In Europe, witches, ghosts and devils are common. In the Caribbean, people dress in African masks and costumes. In Brazil, elaborate costumes are designed and take months to make.

Follow this by . . .

. . . having your own carnival procession wearing your masks and singing a carnival song, such as 'Everybody Loves Carnival Night' in *Tinderbox* (Barratt and Hodge), see Resources list.

Something to think about . . .

What are the special times when you like to have a party with your friends?

ACTIVITY 2 SPRING CLEANING

You will need . . .

. . . dusters, cleaning cloths.

Start by . . .

. . . explaining that spring is the traditional time when people clean their homes after the long dark winter. You could read the beginning of *The Wind in the Willows*, by Kenneth Grahame, where Mole spring cleans his home.

Then . . .

. . . decide together how you could organize a classroom spring clean, for example tidying up and cleaning classroom equipment, washing out paint pots and brushes or washing things in the home corner.

Follow this by . . .

. . . explaining that during Lent, Christians have a 'spring clean' and 'sort out', not just in their homes, but also by thinking about their lives and how they could be better people. They say sorry for the things they know they have done wrong and believe that God will forgive them. It is like being able to have a fresh start in their lives.

Sing the 'Spring Cleaning Rap' from *Spring Tinderbox* (Deshpande and Eccleshare), see Resources list.

Something to think about . . .

When you have tidied up and sorted out your toys and games, do you feel better for having done it?

ACTIVITY 3 MOTHERING SUNDAY

Mothering Sunday is the fourth Sunday in Lent and is a time when the solemn mood of the season is lifted for this festival day. Traditionally it was the time when Christians would make the journey from their own church to the cathedral – their Mother Church. This custom of honouring the Mother Church has been extended to include giving thanks for our own mothers.

You will need . . .

. . . the ingredients for making biscuits (see your favourite cookery book), biscuit cutters in a variety of shapes, coloured icing (this can be bought ready-made), a large sheet of sugar paper cut into the shape of a church.

Start by . . .

. . . discussing with the children the way in which our mothers care for us and look after us. Explore the ways in which 'mothering' is something we can all do, for our friends, our families, in our schools and in our communities.

Then . . .

. . . explain that Christians believe that God loves them and is like a mother who looks after them. In their everyday lives, Christians try to care for each other in a similar way. Sometimes they also describe their church as being like a mother. On Mothering Sunday Christians say thank you to God for their mothers and for their Mother Church.

Follow this by . . .

. . . cooking biscuits to take home for Mum or someone special. Roll out the dough and cut out the biscuits. When they are cooked they can be decorated with the coloured icing. Display them on the sugar paper cut into the shape of a church.

Something to think about . . .

What sort of things does your Mum do for you?

How could you help your Mum more?

Easter

It will help to know that . . .

While Christmas is probably the most well-known Christian festival, Easter is the most important. It is often identified, however, as one of the most challenging aspects of Christianity to teach. In these activities Easter is introduced within the context of the biblical accounts, to emphasize the significance of these for Christians, to draw from them some central Easter themes and to identify some key celebrations in the Christian Church from Palm Sunday to Easter Day.

The Gospels each give detailed accounts of the Easter story and these form the basis of the Christian belief that Jesus came back to life three days after his death on the cross. These beliefs give the focus for Christian worship during Holy Week and Easter. Easter customs, rituals and symbols also try to give meaning and expression to the Christian beliefs about death and resurrection. Some churches, for example, are stripped of decoration until Easter Day when they are filled with flowers and lighted candles to remind Christians of their belief that Jesus, the light of the world, rose from the dead. The natural world is also seen to hold a wealth of symbolic references that demonstrate the central Christian beliefs about Easter. The dawn of a new day, the cycle of the seasons and patterns of growth and change are a powerful reminder for Christians of the new life promised by the resurrection.

Easter itself is a movable feast (the date is not fixed in the calendar) but the events of the Easter story are commemorated on the days of the week on which the original events took place – the crucifixion on a Friday (Good Friday) and the resurrection on a Sunday (Easter Day).

Key ideas . . .

◆   Easter is the most important Christian festival.
◆   Christians commemorate Jesus' death on Good Friday.
◆   Christians believe that Jesus came back to life. This is celebrated on Easter Day.
◆   The cross is the world-wide symbol for Christians.

The Bible can help you . . .

Each of the Gospels has an account of Jesus' entry into Jerusalem (Palm Sunday). See Matthew 21.1-9, Mark 11.1-10, Luke 19.28-38 and John 12.12-15. The death and resurrection of Jesus is recorded in Matthew 27 and 28, Mark 15 and 16, Luke 23 and 24, and John 19 and 20.

Key words . . .

crown, palm, cross, crown of thorns, crucifixion, resurrection, new life

ACTIVITY 1 CROWNS FOR A KING

> Jesus journeyed to Jerusalem, where he spent the last few days of his life. On his arrival he was greeted like a great hero. As he rode through the streets on a donkey, crowds cheered him and waved palm branches. His appearance in Jerusalem was like that of a new king. By the end of the week, the mood had changed; Jesus had been crucified as a common criminal, wearing a crown of thorns. This contrast in mood is reflected in the following two activities, which could be undertaken separately, but are designed to work as a pair.

A Palm Sunday crown

You will need . . .

. . . card, green paper, scissors, glue.

Start by . . .

. . . asking the children if they have ever been in a large crowd of people, for example, at a football match, a pantomime or a circus. Have they joined in with the shouting or singing of songs, calling out the name of their hero, and participating when the crowd is expected to join in with the fun? Encourage them to share their experiences of how it felt to be part of the crowd.

Then . . .

. . . explain that Jesus was welcomed as a hero when he arrived in Jerusalem. Tell the story about Jesus' triumphal entry into the city. Encourage the children to imagine what it was like to be part of the crowd on that day. Everyone was expecting him to be the new leader. It was like welcoming a new king who was going to save them. The crowd shouted out 'Hosanna' (save us, we pray) and waved palm branches. Christians remember this event each year on Palm Sunday.

Something to think about . . .

What words or pictures would you use for a banner to welcome Jesus?

What song would you sing to welcome an important visitor to your school?

Follow this by . . .

. . . making a crown of palm leaves. Cut out palm shaped leaves and on each one write the word 'Hosanna'. Attach the palm leaves to a band of card and adjust this to fit the child's head. Have your own procession wearing the crowns and singing a Palm Sunday song, for example, 'Hosanna, hosanna' (no. 365 in *Junior Praise*, see Resources list).

A Good Friday crown

You will need . . .

. . . long, thin twigs or stems without any foliage (you need to be able to bend these easily without them snapping – honeysuckle and ivy stems, stripped of their leaves, work well).

Start by . . .

. . . reminding the children that on Palm Sunday Jesus was welcomed into Jerusalem like a king. Just a few days later Jesus had become very unpopular with the religious leaders, who thought that he was very dangerous. They hated him so much that they wanted to get rid of him. They dressed him in a purple robe, the colour worn by kings, but they made him wear a crown of thorns as a way of making fun of him. He was killed in a very cruel way: they nailed him to a cross and left him to die.

Then . . .

. . . explain that Christians remember these events on Good Friday. Make a display using the symbols of Good Friday. The crown of thorns can be made by binding together the bare stems into a crown shape. Place this on a piece of purple cloth. You could also add to this a cross or crucifix.

Follow this by . . .

. . . explaining that Good Friday is the saddest day of the Christian year, when Christians remember that Jesus suffered a very cruel death. The crown of thorns is a reminder that Jesus had to suffer a lot of pain. Even though this is a very sad time, Christians believe this is not the end of the story. They know they can look forward to Easter Day and the promise of new life.

Something to think about . . .

What things make you feel sad?

How do you feel when someone hurts you?

ACTIVITY 2   GROWING AN EASTER GARDEN

Creating an Easter garden is a way of illustrating the events of the Easter story as they unfold. Familiarize yourself with the key points of the story before you begin. It is satisfying if you begin the activity at the beginning of Lent. The final touches to the Easter garden are then added just before the Easter holidays.

You will need . . .

. . . a metal tray or old baking tin, potting compost, grass seeds, twigs or lolly sticks, small stones or pebbles, gravel, spring flowers, e.g. primroses, crocuses and miniature spring bulbs.

Start by . . .

. . . filling your container with potting compost, piling the compost into a mound at one corner. In another corner pile the stones and pebbles to form the 'tomb'. Plant the grass seed, to cover the whole of your garden, at the beginning of Lent. Keep it well watered and then watch it grow. A pair of scissors can be used to trim the grass and keep it in order. Explain to the children that the garden they are creating is going to help them to find out about, and to tell, the story of Easter.

Then . . .

. . . when the grass has covered your garden, tell the story of Easter. (The resource list gives some examples of appropriate retellings of the story.) The different areas of the garden can then be created.

◆   Make three crosses by binding together the twigs. Place them on the mound of grass.

◆   Create a gap in the pile of stones representing the tomb. Find a rounded pebble to stand by the entrance.

◆   Use the gravel to make a winding path from the crosses to the tomb.

◆   Plant the spring flowers around the edge of your garden.

Follow this by . . .

. . . encouraging the children to recall the story of Easter using the garden to help them.

Something to think about . . .

What are the signs of new life that you see around you in the spring?

ACTIVITY 3 AN EASTER TREE

You will need . . .

. . . twigs and branches from trees that are not in leaf, tissue paper to make paper flowers, pieces of egg shaped card, fine thread or ribbon.

Start by . . .

. . . looking at the branches and finding words to describe them, e.g. bare, dead and lifeless.

Then . . .

. . . make tissue paper flowers and decorate the paper eggs with bright colours and symbols of new life. In Russia, Poland and other Eastern European countries, eggs are traditionally painted with bold, brightly coloured designs.

Follow this by . . .

. . . making the bare branches into an Easter tree by tying the paper flowers and eggs to the tree branches. This makes your tree 'come alive' with life and colour. The Easter tree is a powerful, visual expression of the Easter story and its central theme of death and resurrection.

Something to think about . . .

How do some trees look different at different times of the year?

How does a tiny acorn become a massive oak tree?

ACTIVITY 4   THE CROSS

You will need . . .

. . . twigs, string or wool, thick green card, small pebbles, stones, clay or modelling material, crêpe paper.

Start by . . .

. . . reading the story *The Tale of Three Trees* (Hunt) or watching either of the videos *Freddie the Leaf* (Educational Media International) or *The Proud Tree* (see Resources list).

Then . . .

. . . explain that the cross is important for Christians not only at Easter but at all times, because it reminds them of how Jesus died. This was a very cruel death but they believe Jesus loved them so much he was prepared to die for them. This was not the end of the story, because Christians believe he came back to life.

Something to think about . . .

Where have you seen crosses used, for example, in your school, in the area around your school or worn as jewellery?

Why do you think some Christians wear a cross?

Follow this by . . .

. . . making Easter crosses by tying two twigs together into the shape of a cross. Working on a base of green card, fix the cross to the base with clay or modelling material. Push stones into the clay around the base of the cross, and fix tissue paper flowers between the stones.

 # The Trinity

It will help to know that . . .

. . . Christians believe that God is revealed to them in three ways – God the Father, God the Son and God the Holy Spirit – yet remains one God. Whilst Christianity is one of many faiths that believe in one God, it is this belief in God as three modes of existence that is a distinctive feature of Christianity.

This central belief of Christianity developed in the early church, and it was the way Christians tried to explain the relationship between God, Jesus Christ and the Holy Spirit. This was later defined in the statement of faith at the Council of Nicaea in AD 325. This statement, the Nicene Creed, is still used by Christians today in their worship. Christians say:

We believe in one God, the Father, the almighty, maker of heaven and earth . . .

This describes God as a creator. The image of God as a father has had a lasting significance to the Christian faith down the ages.

We believe in one Lord, Jesus Christ, the only Son of God . . .

Christians assert that Jesus is both human, yet also divine; this was the way in which God experienced what it was to be human.

We believe in the Holy Spirit, the Lord, the giver of life . . .

For Christians, the Holy Spirit is the power of God, which people experience in their daily lives. It is 'God in us', God the sustainer and God the encourager.

This way of trying to make sense of the doctrine of the Trinity might be thought of as a matter of intellectual curiosity, but down the ages Christians have looked for ways of talking about their experience of God, without doing an injustice to the majesty and the all-embracing might that this word entails. The doctrine of the Trinity is one result of this searching, and it remains a mystery that God can be the Father, the Son and the Holy Spirit all at the same time.

Key ideas . . .

◆ Christians believe there is one God who is described in three ways – God the Father, God the Son and God the Holy Spirit.

◆ Christians use a variety of symbols to represent the three different ways of knowing God.

The Bible can help you . . .

In Matthew 28.19 Jesus commands his disciples to baptize people everywhere 'in the name of the Father, the Son, and the Holy Spirit'. In 2 Corinthians 13.14 Paul ends his letter to the Christians at Corinth with 'the grace of the Lord Jesus Christ, the love of God, and the fellowship of the Holy Spirit be with you all'.

Key words . . .

Father, Son, Holy Spirit, symbol

ACTIVITY 1   THREE IN ONE

You will need . . .

. . . circles of card, cocktail sticks, clover or shamrock leaves (or pictures of these).

Start by . . .

. . . encouraging the children to use their own ways of describing what they think God might be like. Explain that Christians describe God in three different ways:

◆   as God the creator of the world;

◆   as Jesus, his Son, born into a human family;

◆   as the Holy Spirit, the part of God that Christians believe is in all people.

Even though Christians use different names, they are describing the same God.

Then . . .

. . . show the children ways in which Christians have used symbols to illustrate the idea of 'three in one'. Examples from nature include a clover leaf or a shamrock leaf, where three leaf segments grow from one stem. Artists have also illustrated the Trinity by showing God the Father holding his Son Jesus, with a dove, representing the Holy Spirit, hovering overhead. Examples of paintings showing the Trinity in the National Gallery can be viewed in their CD ROM *Art Gallery* (Microsoft), which includes images of:

◆   The Coronation of the Virgin Mary (Jacopo di Cione);

◆   The Trinity with Christ crucified (unknown Austrian artist);

◆   The Trinity with Saints (Pesellino and Filippo Lippi).

Follow this by . . .

. . . making a spinning top by taking a circle of card, and dividing it into three equal segments. Write 'Father' on one segment, 'Son' on the second, and 'Holy Spirit' on the third.

Each segment could be coloured differently. Spin the top and watch the separate names of God merge together as one. No matter which way the top lands it will always show one of the Trinity.

Something to think about . . .

Why do Christians say the following words when they meet together?

The grace of our Lord Jesus Christ, and the love of God and the fellowship of the Holy Spirit, be with us all evermore. Amen.

ACTIVITY 2 SAME BUT DIFFERENT

The idea of the Trinity is a complex one that Christians have tried to explain by analogy, metaphor and symbol. Sometimes the symbols can say more than words. Exploring the properties of water as liquid, solid (ice) and gas (steam) is a way of illustrating that the same thing can exist in three different forms. It can be a useful parallel when exploring the Trinity.

You will need . . .

. . . ice cubes, a jug of water, a kettle.

Start by . . .

. . . discussing what might happen to water when it is heated and cooled. Then discover together that water exists as liquid, ice and steam. Boil a kettle and watch the water turn to steam, freeze water to make ice and then watch the ice cubes melt and turn back to water. You could combine your activity with some science!

Then . . .

. . . encourage the children to record their discoveries about what has happened to the water and how it changes when it is heated and cooled.

Follow this by . . .

. . . exploring the idea that water exists in three different states. In a similar way, Christians believe God is present for them in three different forms.

ACTIVITY 3 A TIME TO GROW

The Christian calendar is made up of a pattern of festivals and seasons. The season of Trinity, beginning with Trinity Sunday, has traditionally been seen as a time when Christians grow in their understanding of God as Father, Son and Holy Spirit. Green is the colour used in the Trinity season. It is naturally associated with this season of growth, and in many churches green is used to decorate the altar and for the priests' garments.

You will need . . .

. . . model making materials, cress seeds and blotting paper.

Start by . . .

. . . asking the children if they know the names of any Christian festivals, e.g. Christmas or Easter. Explain that Trinity Sunday is a special festival day and the period following this is when Christians think about the three aspects of God (Father, Son and Holy Spirit).

Then . . .

. . . design and make a Trinity symbol. The Trinity has traditionally been illustrated in many different ways – a common one is the symbol of an interwoven circular pattern. It is in three parts but, significantly, there is no obvious beginning or ending. For Christians, this represents God's everlasting love. Use this to make models, badges and plaques using clay or modelling material.

Follow this by . . .

. . . making the Trinity pattern by planting cress seeds on damp blotting paper. Then watch your Trinity symbol grow!

Special meals

It will help to know that . . .

We have all experienced the pleasure of sharing a meal with friends. It is a social occasion that unites us, and is something with universal appeal. Not only is it a very natural thing to want to do, it also reinforces our communal life, and affirms us within our family or circle of friends.

The sharing of food within a social setting is as old as society itself, and there are many references to this type of activity within the Judeo-Christian story. There are also many references to the sharing of food with strangers as well as with family.

Not only is food important for all humans on a regular basis in order to sustain life, there are also times when meals are singled out as having special significance to mark particular times in people's lives – the 'wedding breakfast' or a 'birthday party', for example. There are also important times within the religious calendar when special meals are prepared. In the Jewish community, the Passover meal is of great significance, as this is when Jewish people remember their escape from oppression in Egypt.

For Christians, the sharing of bread and wine is of great significance. This service is called by various names, for example, Eucharist, Holy Communion, Mass or The Lord's Supper. The Gospels make it clear that when Jesus instituted this meal it was part of the Passover celebrations. This took place in Jerusalem just before Jesus' death when he met with his disciples to share the Passover meal. Christians refer to this as the Last Supper. The ritual of the Eucharist follows the instruction given by Jesus to his disciples at the Last Supper, when he told them to share bread and wine together, whenever they met for worship, to remember him.

Key ideas . . .

◆   People share meals to mark special occasions.

◆   Christians share bread and wine together, when they worship, to remember Jesus.

The Bible can help you . . .

. . . in the New Testament there are four accounts of the institution of the Eucharist – one by Saint Paul in 1 Corinthians 11.23-25 and three in the Gospels of Matthew 26.26-28, Mark 14.22-24 and Luke 22.17-20.

Key words . . .

Eucharist, saying thank you, bread, wine

ACTIVITY 1 COME TO THE PARTY

> These activities could be undertaken separately but have been designed as a set of three and would work best if carried out in the order presented here.

You will need . . .

. . . a large box containing a table setting for a children's party (a tablecloth, decorated paper plates and cups, table decorations, napkins and party hats), some special food, e.g. fairy cakes.

Start by . . .

. . . unpacking the box and laying a table as for a party.

Then . . .

. . . encourage the children to discuss the ways in which special meals are prepared and draw out the differences between these preparations and those for an ordinary meal. Talk about:

◆   the special table decorations;

◆   the special clothes worn, e.g. party hats, new clothes;

◆   the special food to be eaten.

Follow this by . . .

. . . making plans for a special party together. You could design your own party hats and table decorations and decide what special foods to prepare.

Something to think about . . .

When do you have special meals?

What do you like to eat at them?

ACTIVITY 2 A SPECIAL MEAL FOR CHRISTIANS

This activity could form part of a visit to your local church but can be carried out successfully in the classroom. Why not ask a minister to help you? She/he would probably be able to supply all the things you need. If you invite the minister to help you, don't forget to ask him/her to bring the clothes he/she wears at the Eucharist service.

You will need . . .

. . . a large box containing the artefacts to celebrate the Eucharist (a white tablecloth, a chalice (the goblet used for wine), a paten (the plate used for the bread), a bread roll and some red grape juice to represent wine.

Start by . . .

. . . unpacking the box and carefully placing the objects on the white tablecloth. Just as the table for a special party meal is carefully prepared, Christians also make careful preparations for a special meal. You may want to introduce one of the names used for the meal, e.g. Eucharist, Mass or The Lord's Supper.

Then . . .

. . . tell the story of the events of the Last Supper, using this outline.

◆ Just before his death, Jesus had a special meal with his friends.

◆ Jesus shared bread and wine with them.

◆ He told his friends to do this when they met together.

◆ By doing this they would remember him.

Follow this by . . .

. . . explaining that Christians continue to remember Jesus when they share bread and wine together at the Eucharist. Encourage the children to look closely at the objects used for the Eucharist. Make close observation drawings.

Something to think about . . .

How do you remember important times, for example, do you take photographs of special occasions or special people?

ACTIVITY 3 BREAD TO SHARE

You will need . . .

. . . cooking facilities.

Start by . . .

. . . assembling these ingredients:

680g (or 1 ½ lb) strong white bread flour

1 level tablespoon sugar

2 level teaspoons salt

3 level teaspoons dried active bolding yeast

14g (or ½ oz) fat or oil (optional)

400 ml (14 fl oz) 'hand hot' water

This will be enough to make two small loaves (two 1 lb tins).

Then . . .

. . . follow this recipe to make the bread.

1. Put the flour into a large mixing bowl and stand somewhere warm.

2. Dissolve 1 teaspoon of the sugar in $\frac{1}{3}$ of the water. Add the yeast and whisk. Stand in a warm place until frothy (this will take about ten minutes).

3. Rub the fat into the flour.

4. Dissolve the rest of the sugar and salt into the remaining water and add this and the yeast to the flour.

5. Mix until a smooth dough is formed. Knead it on a floured board until it is no longer sticky (this will take about five minutes).

6. Cover the dough and leave it in a warm place for twenty minutes to prove.

7. Turn the dough onto a floured board and knead. Divide dough in half. Make each piece into a ball and then shape and put into greased tins (at this stage preheat your oven).

8. Cover the tins and leave them in a warm place until the dough is half an inch above the top of the tins (this will take about twenty minutes).

9. Bake at 450°F (232°C) or gas mark 8 for 30 to 35 minutes.

Something to think about . . .

What favourite foods would you like to share with your friends?

Follow this by . . .

. . . explaining that Christians share bread when they meet together. In their worship the bread is broken and given to everyone. Christians feel close to Jesus when they share bread, because they are doing what Jesus did with his friends.

Special occasions

It will help to know that . . .

Just as we mark important times, such as birthdays and anniversaries, particular times in a Christian's life are marked by special occasions. These occasions are shared with other members of the faith community and centre upon an act of worship.

Baptism

The words 'baptize' and 'christen' are interchangeable. Both refer to the ceremony that admits people into the Christian Church. The tradition is as old as Christianity itself. Jesus was baptized by his cousin, John the Baptist, in the River Jordan, and Christians have continued to be baptized ever since. The practice varies greatly in different traditions; in some, babies are baptized soon after birth, in others, it is considered important that the individual him- or herself makes the baptismal promise when they feel able to do so.

There are common elements used in all styles of baptism; water is used as a sign of cleansing and washing away of sins, and the sign of the cross refers to belonging to Jesus and following his example. In some traditions holy oil is used and candles are lit to symbolize the presence of Jesus. When children are baptized, it is usual for godparents to be chosen from among the family's friends and relations. The godparents' role is to support the parents in bringing up the child in the Christian Church.

Key ideas about Baptism . . .

- People are received into the Christian Church through baptism.
- Water and the sign of the cross are symbols of baptism.
- Both children and adults can be baptized.

The Bible can help you . . .

In the Gospels we read that Jesus was baptized by John the Baptist – see Matthew 3.13-16, Mark 1.9-11 and Luke 3.21-22. After his resurrection Jesus told his disciples to go and baptize people 'in the name of the Father, the Son, and the Holy Spirit' – see Matthew 28.19. In the Acts of the Apostles and the Letters there are numerous references to people being baptized as they enter into the Christian faith.

Key words . . .

water, light, welcome

Marriage

Many marriages take place in church and some children will have attended a marriage service, perhaps as a bridesmaid or a page boy. A Christian marriage service is essentially a Service of Blessing when two people publicly commit themselves to each other for the rest of their lives. The wedding ring is a symbol of everlasting love. A wedding is an occasion that many couples want to share with friends and family.

Key ideas about marriage . . .

◆ Christians believe it is important to marry in church.

◆ There is a special marriage service used by Christians.

The Bible can help you . . .

The most famous biblical story concerning marriage is found in John 2.1-12. In this Bible story Jesus performed the miracle of turning water into wine at a marriage feast at Cana.

Key words . . .

love, ring, promise, wedding

Funeral

Christians have often thought of their lives as a journey. Their earthly life is only part of this journey and it continues after death. Christians believe that when they die they will come closer to God in heaven. Although this is a sad time of parting, memories of happy times shared can be a source of comfort. Memories of the departed are kept alive by tending the grave or memorial, lighting candles on the anniversary of the death and saying prayers of thanksgiving for the life of the loved one.

Key ideas about funerals . . .

◆   Christians hold a funeral service to mark the death of a person.

◆   Christians believe that after a person's death, there is life with God. This is often described as being with God in heaven.

The Bible can help you . . .

The Christian belief in eternal life is expressed by Jesus in John 11.25-6 and also in John 3.16.

Key words . . .

death, saying goodbye, memories, heaven

ACTIVITY 1   WE WELCOME YOU!

> This activity explores infant baptism. Ideally, you will be in a church standing around a font, but it is also feasible to do this activity in the classroom. Wherever you are, why not ask your local minister to help you?

You will need . . .

. . . the font, filled with water (if you do this activity in church) or a bowl filled with water (if you do this activity in school) and a doll.

Start by . . .

. . . explaining to the children that we all belong to particular communities (our immediate family, our school, perhaps the Beavers and Cubs or Rainbows and Brownies, etc.) and that there is often a ceremony to mark the time when we join. Baptism is the way of joining the Christian family.

Then . . .

. . . select a suitable name for your doll, which will be used at its baptism. Explain to the children that water was used to baptize Jesus, and Christians have been following this practice ever since.

'Baptize' the doll by making the sign of the cross on its forehead and then pouring water onto its head. Tell the children that a minister would say the following words:

(Name) . . . I baptize you in the name of the Father and of the Son and of the Holy Spirit. Amen.

Follow this by . . .

. . . thinking about pictures and symbols you could use for a card to give to a baby who is going to be baptized. Design and make some baptism cards.

Something to think about . . .

Have you been to see a baby baptized?

Why do you think it is such a special day for a family and friends to remember?

ACTIVITY 2 WEDDING BELLS

This activity explores Christian marriage. Ideally, you will be in a church but it is also feasible to do this activity in the classroom. Wherever you are, why not ask your local minister to help you? The marriage ceremony is a long service, but you could paraphrase significant parts of it.

You will need . . .

. . . children to take the parts of the principal people at a marriage service, for example, priest or minister, bride, groom, best man, bride's father, bridesmaids, page boys, guests. Don't forget the rings!

Start by . . .

. . . explaining to the children that Christians think it is important to make their marriage promises in church. They believe that they are not just doing this with their family and friends but, most significantly, in the presence of God.

Then . . .

. . . act out a marriage ceremony. Include the following:

◆   the procession into the church;

◆   the wedding vows, e.g. I (*Name*) take you (*Name*) to be my wedded husband/wife;

◆   the priest/minister blessing the rings;

◆   the exchange of rings;

◆   the procession out of the church.

Something to think about . . .

Have you been to a wedding with your family?

Was the wedding in a church or another religious building?

What was your favourite part of the day?

Follow this by . . .

. . . having a celebratory drink and biscuits! Don't forget to take the photographs.

ACTIVITY 3   REMEMBERING

This activity explores death and the Christian funeral service. It is designed for the classroom. It could effectively be combined with a visit to a church to look at memorials and gravestones. These could be in the churchyard, if there is one, or inside the church itself.

You will need . . .

. . . card, paper, writing and drawing materials, photographs and memorabilia of a Christian who is no longer alive. If it is appropriate, and you feel comfortable with this, choose a person from your family, or someone known to the children. You may prefer to invite a guest to the classroom who is prepared to talk about a dead relative or friend.

Start by . . .

. . . sharing the photographs and memorabilia with the children and using these to build up a picture of what the person was like. Talk about his/her personality and interests, and significant his/her events in his/her life, for example, where he/she was born, where he/she went to school, and where he/she worked. Try to include details of the person's Christian life, for example, when and where he/she was baptized, married, attended church and died.

Then . . .

. . . explain that when a Christian dies:

◆ a special funeral service is held;

◆ their life is remembered;

◆ prayers are said;

◆ everyone gives thanks to God for the person's life.

Follow this by . . .

. . . cutting out a large cross shape from card. Put a photograph of the person you have chosen to remember in the centre. Surround this with the children's descriptions of the person and some significant dates.

◆ (*Name*) was married at St John's Church in 1952.

◆ (*Name*) was a teacher who worked at Coal Hill School.

◆ (*Name*) liked to go fishing.

Something to think about . . .

In what different ways do we remember people, places and special events?

How do the trees and the gardens near your school change during the year?

In what ways do people change as they grow older?

Light

It will help to know that . . .

Light is a symbol of hope for everyone in both the sacred and the secular world. For Christians, light represents the presence of Jesus in the world. The Gospel writers refer to Jesus in this way. In Saint John's Gospel, the writer describes the coming of Jesus as a light shining in the darkness. In this part of the world, the birth of Jesus is celebrated in the depths of winter, and the symbolism of light shining in darkness is a very powerful one. For many Christians, the lighting of candles is an important aspect of worship and of individual devotion.

Examples of this practice include the giving of a candle to a newly baptized person; candles lit when offering personal prayers to God, and in some churches candles are to be found in all parts of the building, and play a significant part in worship.

All Christians try to follow the example of Jesus and live their lives as 'lights shining in the world'. Other world faiths use the symbol of light in various ways; creation stories from many traditions have taken up the idea of the life-giving properties of light, and the way in which it overcomes darkness. In this part of the world, the festivals of Diwali, Hanukkah and Christmas, which fall at the end of our calendar year, have become known as Festivals of Light.

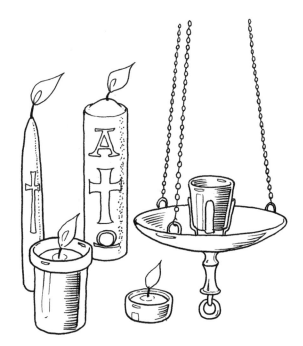

Key ideas . . .

◆ Christians describe Jesus as the light of the world.

◆ Candles are used by Christians to symbolize the presence of Jesus in the world.

◆ Light is a symbol of hope and goodness.

The Bible can help you . . .

In John 1.4-9 and 8.12 Jesus is described as the light of the world. In Matthew 5.14-16 Jesus' followers are also described as the light of the world. In John 3.19, 8.12 and 12.46 Christians read that life without God is darkness.

Key words . . .

symbol, candle, shine, light

ACTIVITY 1   A LIGHT IN THE WORLD

> **Although this activity is quite safe, teachers must take all the usual precautions when dealing with lighted flames in the classroom.**

You will need . . .

. . . religious paintings and pictures, e.g. images on Christmas cards.

Start by . . .

. . . encouraging the children to discuss their experiences of light and darkness, and the feelings that they evoke.

Then . . .

. . . using a famous painting as a stimulus for discussion, explore the way light is used by the artist to identify Jesus as a light in the world. Nativity scenes often show Jesus in a pool of light; artists often identify significant religious figures with haloes, pools of light, shafts of light and stars, etc. The works of artists such as Carravaggio, Rembrandt and Holman Hunt are useful here, as well as the many images found on Christmas cards.

Develop your discussion by ensuring the children are sitting comfortably, and dim the lights in the classroom.

Light the candle and ask the children to describe the effects of the candlelight (for example, on the faces of the people in the room).

Encourage the children to describe the differences they observe between the darkness and the light. How does this make them feel?

Something to think about . . .

How can I help my family and friends today?

Follow this by . . .

. . . introducing the children to the Christian understanding of Jesus being like a light in the world. You could say something like this:

> *Light helps people to see things more clearly. Christians believe that Jesus is like a light shining for them and helping them.*

ACTIVITY 2 REFLECTING LIGHT

You will need . . .

. . . a large cloth or drape to create a dark area, a torch, a range of objects, both natural and manufactured, some of which will sparkle in torchlight.

Start by . . .

. . . exploring the way in which different objects can reflect light.

Then . . .

. . . create a dark area in the corner of the classroom or play space.

◆ Place a range of objects and a torch in the dark area, e.g. natural objects, luminous objects and some with shiny surfaces.

◆ Encourage the children to describe what they see in the torchlight.

◆ Make a collection of words to describe what they saw and how it made them feel.

Follow this by . . .

. . . discussing the wonder and pleasure given by shiny objects, such as precious stones, stars in the sky or sunlight on water. Introduce the idea that Christians try to follow Jesus' example and reflect God's love for all people. For example, just as some objects reflect light, good deeds can bring light into people's lives. By doing good deeds, Christians try to reflect God's light in everything they do.

Something to think about . . .

How can I shine like a star?

ACTIVITY 3 CANDLES

Although this activity is quite safe, teachers must take all the usual precautions when dealing with lighted flames in the classroom.

You will need . . .

. . . a range of different Christian candles, e.g. an Easter candle, a votive candle, an Advent candle and a baptism candle

Start by . . .

. . . discussing the way in which lights are used for celebrations, e.g. birthdays, festivals and ceremonies. You could use a picture of festival illuminations or a fireworks display as a stimulus for your discussion.

Then . . .

. . . make a collection of candles used in Christian worship and use them for close observation drawing.

Make a classroom display of candles used for Christian worship. Your collection could include an Easter candle, a votive candle, an Advent candle and a baptism candle (pupils may be able to contribute to this by bringing in their own baptism candles). Some places of worship, shrines and pilgrimage centres offer candles of various types.

Follow this by . . .

. . . introducing pupils to the various ways in which Christians use candles. If you have a church near to your school, you could arrange a visit to explore this aspect of church life.

Under supervision, the children could light a candle and look closely at the flame, observing its shape, and the different colours in it. Collect words and phrases to describe what they see.

Use the children's drawings and descriptions to add to your display or to make a book of Christian candles.

Something to think about . . .

Light a candle and then think about a person who is special to you.

God's creation

It will help to know that . . .

Humankind has always wondered about how life began and marvelled at nature's ability to rejuvenate itself. The pattern of seasonal change, summer to winter and back again, illustrates the continuous cycle of life, death and renewal, characteristic of the living world. For Christians, the hand of God is seen in this creative process. This is not just a one-off event, but a continuous cycle sustained by God.

Most religious traditions have stories that try to make sense of the beginning of time and of life; timeless stories that speak of people's own experiences and try to explain the inexplicable. Throughout recent history there has been a long-running and lively debate between religion and science about theories of creation. These are often seen as polarized views but they do not have to be mutually exclusive.

Within the Christian community itself there are many shades of opinion. There are those who read the accounts of the beginning of the world in the Bible (Genesis chapters 1 and 2) as literal descriptions. Other Christians, however, see these stories as narratives that describe, in poetic terms, how life began. Views will no doubt continue to change and develop over time, but for all Christians God is a creating, sustaining force revealed in all aspects of the living world.

Key ideas . . .

◆   Christians believe they live in a world created by God.

◆   Creation stories are found in the Bible.

◆   Christians believe that they should care for the created world.

The Bible can help you . . .

The most well-known creation story in the Bible can be found in the Old Testament in Genesis 1–2.4 followed by a second account in Genesis 2.4-end.

Key words . . .

creator, Genesis, beginnings

ACTIVITY 1 IN THE BEGINNING

This is one of the stories taken from the Jewish scriptures, which were adopted by Christians in the books of the Bible they call the Old Testament. You may like to explore some of the many other creation stories from other religious and cultural traditions around the world, in addition to the one used for this activity.

You will need . . .

. . . seven large sheets of card, collage or painting materials.

Start by . . .

. . . introducing the story of creation from Genesis 1, which describes how God created the world in six days then, satisfied with the work, rested on the seventh day. You could use the outline given below to provide a simple structure.

- On the first day God made light and dark.
- On the second day God made sky and water.
- On the third day God made sea and dry land, and plants and fruits grew on the land.
- On the fourth day God made the sun, the moon and the stars.
- On the fifth day God made fish, sea creatures and birds.
- On the sixth day God made animals and people.
- On the seventh day God rested.

Then . . .

. . . illustrate the events of the seven days using paint and/or collage materials on the seven pieces of card. Label the cards according to what God did on each day.

Follow this by . . .

. . . encouraging the children to tell the story themselves using the pictures as prompts. They could also devise sounds and movements to accompany their story. Have fun!

Something to think about . . .

What kinds of things do you enjoy making?

What sort of world would you like to create?

ACTIVITY 2 CARING FOR GOD'S WORLD

This activity could be carried out at harvest time when Christian churches traditionally set aside a Sunday on which thanks are given for all the fruits of creation and Christians remember their duty to be stewards of God's world.

You will need . . .

. . . cress seeds or other fast growing seeds, egg shells, cotton wool.

Start by . . .

. . . decorating the egg shells with faces or patterns and then filling them with cotton wool. Sprinkle a few seeds onto the surface of the cotton wool and then dampen it with water. The egg shells could be stored in egg boxes on a warm, light windowsill. Keep them well watered and they should start to grow within a couple of days.

Then . . .

. . . keep a record of the seeds as they grow. Put one egg shell to one side and do not water it. The children can then see that without water the seeds will not germinate and grow.

Follow this by . . .

. . . explaining that all living things need to be cared for, fed and watered. Christians believe that they should look after and care for animals and plants, because they are all part of God's creation.

Sing a song about caring for God's world (examples in *Big Blue Planet* (Jarvis), see Resources list).

Something to think about . . .

What do plants and animals need as well as water to help them grow?

Why must we be careful not to waste water?

ACTIVITY 3 ALL THINGS BRIGHT AND BEAUTIFUL

You will need . . .

. . . sewing materials, e.g. embroidery cotton or wool, needles, Binca or rough hessian, examples of Celtic patterns – *The Celtic Resource Book* (Wallace) is a good source (see Resources list).

Start by . . .

. . . showing the children some examples of Celtic patterns. Ask them to try to find where the patterns begin and where they end. Celtic designs are usually regular but characteristically they do not have a recognizable beginning or end point.

Christians believe that God's love has no beginning and no ending – it is always there. Celtic artists use patterns like these, with no apparent beginning or ending, to try to describe this. Sometimes pictures can say more than words!

Then . . .

. . . design patterns where you cannot find the beginning or the end. Copy these onto the Binca or hessian and sew the designs. Or, you could copy a simple Celtic pattern.
Traditional Celtic designs often feature birds or animals. These shapes could be cut from fabric or felt and added to the line pattern.

Follow this by . . .

. . . displaying your designs with the words of a Celtic prayer (see *The Celtic Resource Book* (Wallace) for examples).

Something to think about . . .

How can I look after our beautiful world?

What are the ways in which some people damage our beautiful world?

# Saints

It will help to know that . . .

From the earliest days of the Christian Church, saints have played an important role. The word 'saint' comes from a Latin word meaning holy. The early Christians saw themselves as a community of saints or holy people, but also singled out those individuals who showed outstanding qualities of holiness.

Sainthood was, and still is, established by a process of canonization. In earlier times this was rather haphazard, and relied largely on popular acclaim, but as time went on, a much more rigorous process was established. This process is now formalized, and relies heavily on historical evidence in distinguishing between legendary and authentic aspects of saints' lives.

Saints have often been extremely colourful characters attracting a cult following. It is useful for children to know their stories and recognize them as 'heroes of the faith' – people who show a heroic and single-minded devotion to Christ. Particular days in the Christian calendar are set aside to remember the life and work of individual saints.

The other aspect of sainthood is that Christians believe everyone has the potential for holiness, so we are all saints in the making! It is on All Saints' Day that Christians remember those who have followed the teachings of Jesus, and who, they believe, are now in heaven. This festival is celebrated on 1 November.

Key ideas . . .

◆ Particular individuals are commemorated as saints as recognition of their exemplary Christian lives.

◆ The word 'saint' can be used to describe all Christians.

The Bible can help you . . .

The New Testament does not use the title 'saint' for particular people. It does, however, frequently use the word to describe Christians, for example, in Romans 1.7 and Philippians 4.21.

Key words . . .

holiness, special people, festival days

Activity 1 All Saints

> Although this activity is quite safe, teachers must take all the usual precautions when dealing with lighted flames in the classroom.

You will need . . .

. . . several sheets of thin A4 card, the same number of sheets of acetate paper, acetate pens, a jam jar with a night-light in it.

Start by . . .

. . . cutting 5 cm diameter holes in the card (about ten in each A4 sheet) and then glue the acetate paper to the back of it, taking care not to get glue over the holes.

Then . . .

. . . get the children to draw a picture of their face on the acetate paper with acetate pen, explaining that Christians believe that just as Jesus is known as the light of the world (see Light, activity 1, p. 55) so they believe there is a bit of God in each of them – they are all saints – and they must shine as lights, too.

Something to think about . . .

Have you done anything today which is saint-like?

Follow this by . . .

. . . making the card into a tube, lighting the night-light and placing it in the jam jar. Slip the tube over the jar so the pictures of the children's faces shine through with the light at the back of them.

Activity 2 Saint Francis

You will need . . .

. . . pieces of paper 10 cm square, pencils and colouring materials, a dish or tin.

Start by . . .

. . . asking the children what their favourite toys are. Then on separate pieces of paper, draw and name them. Gather the children into a circle and ask each in turn to tell the rest of the group about their favourite toy.

Then . . .

. . . tell the story of how Saint Francis, a rich young man, gave away all his possessions. You may want to use this outline.

◆   Francis was the son of a wealthy cloth merchant.

◆   When he was young he was very rich and led a carefree life.

◆   One day he had a vision that Jesus told him to repair the church at San Damiano.

◆   He sold a bale of cloth from his father's warehouse to pay for repairing the church.

◆   His father was very cross and disowned him.

◆   Francis gave away all his money and went away penniless to become a friar (monk).

Something to think about . . .

How do children feel who have very few toys to play with?

Follow this by . . .

. . . inviting the children to put their pieces of paper into a dish in the middle of the circle. Ask them to imagine what it would be like to give away the real thing. How would they feel about this?

ACTIVITY 3   SAINT JULIAN

You will need . . .

. . . a number of small and beautiful natural objects (e.g. sea shells, flowers and nuts), one for each person in the group

Start by . . .

. . . telling the children about Julian of Norwich.

◆   Lady Julian of Norwich spent most of her life alone in a cell next to a church in Norwich.

◆   She had a vision and heard God speaking to her.

Then . . .

. . . give the children the opportunity to choose one of the objects on the table. Give them time to hold the object in their hands and to observe it closely. Explain that this is what Julian saw in her dream, and when she woke up she had three things to say about the little object in her hand. Julian believed that:

◆ God had made this little object.

◆ God loves the little object.

◆ God cares for it.

Follow this by . . .

. . . getting the children to draw and paint the object they have chosen. Encourage them to look at it very closely.

Something to think about . . .

If God made, loves and looks after such a simple thing as a shell, does God do the same for me?

 # Mary

It will help to know that . . .

. . . the Mother of Jesus has always held a very special place in the Christian story. Very little is known about her own background and less still about her husband Joseph.

The little information we have about Mary is found in the Gospels of Matthew and Luke. In these accounts Mary is told by an angel that she is to have a baby who is God's son.

At various strategic points in the gospel story, Mary is mentioned by name – at a wedding feast at Cana in Galilee and, more importantly, when Jesus was put to death on the cross. There Jesus put her into the care of Saint John, whom he tells to treat Mary as his own mother.

Mary's influence and importance varies considerably depending on the tradition. For example, Roman Catholics and Orthodox Christians value Mary as a central focus in their worship, while others would want to stress her humility, and react against what they consider her glorification.

The figure of Mary is a very important one for Christians in Latin America. In Mexico, the Virgin of Guadalupe represents the Indian people, and the key text of the Magnificat (see Activity 2) is an important one in understanding Mary as representing the poor and oppressed people of the world – a world where God brings 'down mighty kings from their thrones' and lifts 'up the lowly'.

There are several important feast days for Mary during the year, which mark important events in her life. These include her birth (8 September), the time when the Angel Gabriel announced that she was to be the Mother of God – the Annunciation (25 March) and when she took Jesus to be presented at the Temple at Jerusalem – the Presentation (2 February).

Key ideas . . .

◆   Mary is the Mother of Jesus and is referred to as the Mother of God.

◆   Mary is a very important saint for Christians throughout the world.

◆   Mary obeyed God, even though it was very difficult for her.

The Bible can help you . . .

In Luke 1.26-38 the angel Gabriel tells Mary she is going to have a baby (the Annunciation) and Mary responds by singing the Magnificat (verses 46–55); in Luke 2.1-7 and Matthew 1.18-25 Mary gives birth to Jesus. Other references to Mary include Luke 2.41-51 when Jesus gets left behind in the Temple at Jerusalem.

Key words . . .

mother, saint, obeying God

ACTIVITY 1 GOOD NEWS

You will need . . .

. . . artists' drawings of the Annunciation (often found on Christmas cards), poster packs, National Gallery CD ROM.

Start by . . .

. . . listening to the children's 'news', e.g. after the weekend/holiday. Discuss with them the importance of telling others about their experiences, both good and bad. Explore with them how we often want to tell others about things that happen to us. Sometimes we want to tell everybody and sometimes we just want to talk to a special friend or perhaps someone in our family.

Then . . .

. . . show the children a picture of the Annunciation as a way of illustrating the story of how Mary received the news that she was going to have a baby.

Follow this by . . .

. . . encouraging the children to make their own pictures and describe in words how they think Mary felt when she received her news. Then display these pictures with their responses.

Something to think about . . .

When you hear some good news, who would you want to tell about it?

ACTIVITY 2 MAGNIFICAT

You will need . . .

. . . chime bars, guitar, piano, xylophones, etc., but these are optional.

Start by . . .

. . . singing this simple chant slowly and with a very steady rhythm. It is a setting of the first words of the song of praise sung by Mary when her cousin Elizabeth had greeted her as the Mother of God. The words are in Latin and translated mean 'My soul magnifies the Lord'.

Then . . .

. . . sing it as a two (or more) part round. The parts enter at B, C and D.

Follow this by . . .

. . . adding the simple chordal accompaniment to the chant, using chime bars or other chordal instruments as well as a piano and a guitar. The bass part uses only four notes repeated over and over again, so it is quite easy to learn.

Something to think about . . .

How does it feel to sing the chant over and over again?

Magnificat

My soul magnifies the Lord

Principal canon

Ma - gni - fi - cat,   Ma - gni - fi - cat,   Ma - gni - fi - cat a - ni - ma

me - a Do - mi - num. Ma - gni - fi - cat, Ma - gni - fi - cat, Ma - gni - fi - cat a - ni - ma me - a!

Accompaniments

Keyboard

Guitar

From *Music From Taizé* (Collins Liturgical Publications, 1984).
Music: Jacques Berthier (1923-1994). Copyright © Ateliers et
Presses de Taizé, 71250 Taizé – Communauté, France.

ACTIVITY 3 THE ROSARY

The practice of saying a prayer a set number of times is an extremely ancient one, and is found in many religious traditions. When using the rosary, The Lord's Prayer ('Our Father . . .') is recited. This is followed by the following prayer:

> *Hail Mary full of grace, the Lord be with you,*
> *blessed are you among women,*
> *and blessed is the fruit of your womb, Jesus.*
> *Holy Mary, pray for us now and at the hour of our death.*

This is repeated ten times, after which the words 'Glory be to the Father' are said.

This is followed by a period of meditation on one of the sorrowful or joyful mysteries of Jesus and his mother's life.

If you know someone who uses the rosary for prayer why not ask him/her to visit you to explain how he/she uses the rosary?

You will need . . .

. . . beads, cotton reels, pasta shapes, wool, strong thread or long laces.

Start by . . .

. . . making a mystery bag (a small cloth bag with a drawstring top). Put a set of rosary beads into it. Pass the mystery bag around for the children to feel, explore and raise questions as to its contents.

Then . . .

. . . slowly reveal the rosary beads and ask how the children think Christians might use them as an aid to prayer. Links could be made with the children's own experience of using beads to count. Explain how the beads are divided into groups of ten to help Christians follow the rosary prayers.

Follow this by . . .

. . . asking the children to design and construct some prayer beads for Christians to use for prayer. Make a display of the different designs.

Something to think about . . .

Why do you think some prayers are said over and over again?

Talking and listening to God

It will help to know that . . .

For those who believe in God, prayer is a natural inclination. It is a way of communicating with and developing a relationship with God.

Christians regard it as very important to 'raise their hearts to God'. Prayer, in a narrow sense of the word, means asking God for the things which will help them. Since very early times, however, prayer has taken on a much broader meaning, and Christians would include praising God and giving thanks for all the good things of this life, as well as saying sorry to God for things they have done wrong.

In the early church, Christians took over the Jewish custom of standing with hands raised high when praying to God with others in acts of worship. They also understood that prayers could be offered silently and privately by individuals, and this has remained an important feature of Christian prayer.

As well as speaking to God in praise, offering thanks and asking for help, Christians believe it is very important to listen and to try to understand what it is that God is saying to them. These themes of praise, thanksgiving and petition, and of talking and listening to God are reflected in the following activities.

Key ideas . . .

◆ Christians pray to God.

◆ Praying is talking and listening to God.

The Bible can help you . . .

There are many examples of people praying to God in the Bible, including Jesus himself. Jesus was asked by his disciples how to pray. This is found in Matthew 6.9-13 and in Luke 11.2-4, and is the source of the Lord's Prayer – the most famous Christian prayer.

Key words . . .

prayer, praise, saying thank you, saying sorry

ACTIVITY 1   A FAMOUS PRAYER

You will need . . .

. . . a large piece of paper with the outline of a head and upper body on it, separate cards each with a line of the prayer written on it (see below), a piece of card cut into the shape of a cross (this will be used for the last line of the prayer).

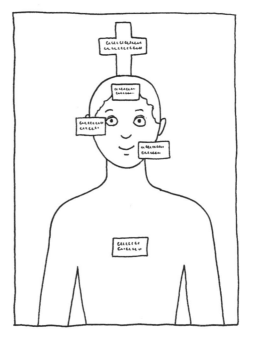

Start by . . .

. . . writing the words of this prayer on a large sheet of card or overhead transparency.

> *God be in my head, and in my understanding;*
> *God be in my eyes, and in my looking;*
> *God be in my mouth, and in my speaking;*
> *God be in my heart, and in my thinking;*
> *God be at my end and at my departing.*

Read the prayer to the children. You may find it helpful to use these words to introduce the prayer: 'This is a well-known prayer that is used by Christians when they talk to God.' Tell the children that this prayer has been used by Christians for hundreds of years.

Then . . .

. . . discuss each line of the prayer with the children, placing the cards on the picture of the head and body as you talk about each one. When Christians say this prayer they are asking God to be with them in all parts of their lives – seeing, speaking and thinking. When you come to the last line place the cross at the top of the picture to show that Christians believe God is with them even when they die.

Something to think about . . .

Why do Christians find it helpful to pray to God?

Do you know any other Christian prayers?

Follow this by . . .

. . . learning the words of this famous prayer. (You might recognize the words as a hymn. The tune by Henry Walford Davies is quite easy to learn and is to be found in most hymn books.)

ACTIVITY 2   LET'S TALK

You will need . . .

. . . three circles of coloured card stuck on to a large sheet of paper (on the first circle of card write 'Thank you . . .', on the second write 'I'm sorry . . .' and on the third write 'Please help . . .'), petal shapes made out of coloured card to match the circles.

Start by . . .

explaining to the children that when Christians pray they:

- ◆   thank God for all the good things in their lives;
- ◆   say sorry to God for the times when they have done things wrong;
- ◆   ask God to help them with any problems they have.

Then . . .

. . . ask the children to think about what Christians would:

- ◆   want to thank God for, e.g. our food, our homes;
- ◆   want to say sorry to God for, e.g. being nasty to our friends;
- ◆   ask for help with, e.g. being kind to each other.

Follow this by . . .

. . . writing these ideas on different coloured petals and then sticking them onto the appropriate circles of card to complete the flower prayers.

Something to think about . . .

Why do we say please and thank you?

When do you say you are sorry?

ACTIVITY 3 LET'S LISTEN

> This activity is devised to help children understand that praying is a two way process; not only do Christians want to speak to God, they also try to listen to what God has to say to them.

You will need . . .

. . . pairs of prompt cards, one with the words: 'Christians want to thank God for . . .' and the other with the word 'Because . . .'

Start by . . .

. . . explaining that when Christians pray, they not only talk to God, but they also listen. You might use the example of sharing news together, when it is important to listen to other people as well as to speak.

Then . . .

. . . as a class activity, try to complete the statements, as shown below.

◆   Christians thank God for the sunshine and the rain.

◆   Christians thank God for the sunshine and the rain because they make the crops grow.

Follow this by . . .

. . . dividing the children into pairs. Give each pair a set of the prompt cards and encourage them to think of some more examples.

Something to think about . . .

When is it important to listen to others?

Visiting a church

These two sections are designed to help you to plan visits to local churches. The first set of activities looks specifically at the church building and the second set concentrates on Christians who use the church for their worship. You might want to use the activities for 'Special occasions' (see pp. 50–53) in conjunction with those in this section, as part of your visit to a church.

It will help to know that . . .

. . . the word 'church' is used both for the building itself and for the local Christian community. It is also sometimes used to describe the world-wide family of Christians.

Church buildings vary greatly in size and appearance. Some are small and quite plain, others are huge and may be richly decorated. The way in which Christians worship in their church also differs widely. The worship may be very simply said by a few people or very complex with great ceremony and music, with a large number of people present. You may have opportunities to explore some of the rich variety of buildings and practice that is available to you in your community. Don't worry if you only have one church in your locality, as every church has something special to offer.

The best people to help you with these activities are members of the faith community who worship regularly at your local church. They will be able to tell you about the history of the church and how it is used today, and explore with the children the ways in which they express their faith. In the following activities, members of the church community are your main resource. By working with people in this way the children are introduced to various aspects of Christian worship.

Church services go on throughout the week but Sunday is the most important day for Christian worship. Christians can worship together at any time, but Sunday has special significance for them, because it is the day on which they believe that Jesus rose from the dead – the Day of Resurrection. Careful preparations are made for worship, at which Christians praise God and give thanks for his love and care for all the world.

Key ideas . . .

◆ The church is a special building set aside for worship, study, teaching and prayer.

◆ Churches are sacred places for Christians.

◆ Sunday is the most important day for Christian worship.

The Bible can help you . . .

In the early days of Christianity, people probably met together in each other's homes for worship. The development of churches as centres for worship came with time and as Christians became more confident about worshipping publicly. In the Gospels Jesus talks about the 'church' only twice. In Matthew 16.18 he explains that the disciple Peter will found a church ' . . . on this rock (that is, the disciple Peter) I will build my church', and also Matthew 18.17 when Jesus speaks of reporting a offending brother to 'the church'.

Many religions mark one day of the week as their special day. For Christians, this day is Sunday. In the book of Revelation this day is referred to as the Lord's day.

Key words . . .

building, community, worship, sacred space, Sunday

The church building

The following three activities may be used on one or more visits to a church. They follow the sequence of:

◆ exploring the outside of the church;

◆ looking at some particular features within the building;

◆ learning about some of the artefacts used in church.

ACTIVITY 1
A SPECIAL PLACE FOR CHRISTIANS

Before your visit . . .

. . . explore the church to which you are going to take the children so you know where the interesting features of the church are. It is essential that you have visited the church prior to your visit with the children and made contact with members of the faith community who work there (see 'Checklist for a visit to a church' on p. 84).

Start by . . .

. . . having a good look at the outside of the building and the church grounds and making a list of the features that mark it out as a special place for Christians.

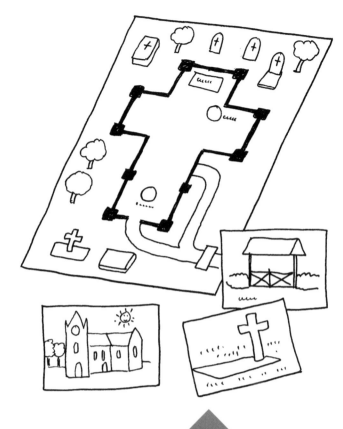

- ◆ Are there crosses in the grounds and on the building?

- ◆ What shape are the windows and the doors?

- ◆ Can you work out the shape of the building?

- ◆ Does it have a tower or steeple?

- ◆ Is there a notice board? What does it tell you about the church and the people who use the building?

Then . . .

. . . ask the children to make a list of all these special features or draw something within the church grounds that they find interesting. You could plot these features on a ground plan.

Follow this by . . .

. . . encouraging the children to think about how this building is different from their home or school, e.g. the shape of the windows and doors, size, building materials, etc.

Links with other faiths

- ◆ Do you know any other special places of worship near to your school?

- ◆ Which buildings are used by different faith communities in your area?

Something to think about . . .

How do people passing by this building know that it is a church?

What do you think you will find inside the building?

ACTIVITY 2   USING YOUR SENSES

Before your visit . . .

. . . negotiate with your church contact ways in which a special atmosphere could be created within the church. If it is the tradition of the church to use candles and incense, could these be alight when the children come into church to create a 'prayerful atmosphere'? Appropriate music, being played softly, is also very helpful.

You will need . . .

. . . nothing! It is important at this stage that the children do not have distractions such as bags and coats and writing materials because the activity relies on them being free to explore their own feelings. You may wish to make a record of some of the children's observations.

Start by . . .

. . . asking the children to come into the church silently, putting all their belongings into a place at the back of the church and finding a space on their own to sit quietly and absorb the atmosphere of the building.

Then . . .

. . . ask them to let their minds wander, to soak up the atmosphere of the space and look around them and notice any of the features of the church that they find unusual or attractive. (The length of time for this activity will vary according to the children's age and ability to sit still.)

Follow this by . . .

. . . gathering the children together, and asking them to talk about how they feel about being in this special place, and to comment on anything they found unusual and interesting. Which 'senses' (sight, hearing, smell . . .) did they use?

Something to think about . . .

Can you think of other buildings that feel special when you go into them?

What is your favourite part of the church? Why?

ACTIVITY 3 THINGS TO LOOK FOR

Styles of worship are reflected in the architecture and layout of your local church building. The key features identified in this activity are given as a guide to the main areas of worship within most Christian communities.

Before your visit . . .

. . . identify the key features of the church building:

◆ cross;

◆ font/place of baptism;

◆ altar/table;

◆ pulpit/reading desk/lectern.

You will need . . .

. . . paper on a clip board and pencils.

Start by . . .

. . . taking the children to each of the places identified and examining them. Explain to the children what each feature is used for. Your church guide will be able to help you with this.

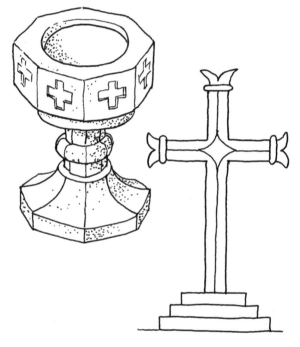

Then . . .

. . . make each of them 'come alive'. For example, at the lectern a child might read a short passage from the Bible; at the font you could find out who has been baptized or if any of the children can remember their baptism or the baptism of one of their family or friends.

Follow this by . . .

. . . allowing some time for the children to make careful sketches of their favourite part of the church, or a detail of it.

Something to think about . . .

What were the special things in the church for you?

What did the atmosphere in the church make you think about?

The church community

The next three activities explore the key roles played by particular Christians within the life of their church. The following activities could take place in school, but they have a clearer focus if they are part of a church visit.

ACTIVITY 1   A DAY IN THE LIFE OF . . .

Start by . . .

. . . asking the vicar/minister/elder of your local church to work with you. Invite him/her to describe the role of a leader within the church.

Then . . .

. . . ask her/him to explain what she/he does when leading the worship in the church. Use these questions as a guide:

- What preparations are made for worship?
- What music will be sung/played?
- What prayers will be said?
- What passage(s) from the Bible will be read in the worship?
- What special clothes are worn during the service?

Something to think about . . .

Why is so much effort put into getting ready for worship?

How do your teachers prepare their lessons for you?

Follow this by . . .

. . . asking your visitor to focus on one or more aspects of his/her work. Encourage the children to record aspects of their discussion in words and pictures. They could compile 'A day in the life of . . .'

ACTIVITY 2   MY JOB IS . . .

Before your visit . . .

. . . contact one of the people within the church community who has a specific job to do in the church. This might be the music leader, the organist, the person who prepares the items for the Eucharist, or a person who cleans the church.

Start by . . .

. . . introducing your guest. Ask him/her to describe what he/she does in the church, and how he/she goes about the job.

Then . . .

. . . encourage the children to ask questions about your guest's work. Use these questions as a guide.

- ◆　Why is your job important for the church?
- ◆　How long does it take to do your job?
- ◆　How long have you been doing your job?
- ◆　What equipment do you use?
- ◆　Do you have anyone to help you?

Something to think about . . .

Would you like to do the job you have just tried?

Why do you think this job is so important for the church?

Follow this by . . .

. . . trying out some of the jobs that have to be done, and then recording some of the children's experiences (don't forget to take the camera).

ACTIVITY 3 SUNDAY

Before your visit . . .

. . . make contact with an established member of the church community who would be willing to talk to the children about why he/she attends church. Your local church leader should be able to recommend an appropriate person to do this.

Start by . . .

. . . asking what is special to your guest about the church. You might then focus the discussion on Sunday worship, to introduce the idea that Sunday is the most important day for Christians.

Something to think about . . .

What are the things that you do every week?

Why do you think Christians like to go to church as often as they can?

Then . . .

. . . through a question and answer session, try to build up a picture of a typical Sunday in the life of the church.

Follow this by . . .

. . . asking the church member to show the children a favourite part of the church (this might be a picture, or a window, for example). If you are in school, your guest could share with the children a favourite story, prayer or song that he/she particularly associates with the church.

Key features of a church

Cross/crucifix

◆ This is the most important symbol for Christians throughout the world.

◆ Some Christians use the empty cross to symbolize the risen Christ.

◆ Some Christians use a crucifix as a reminder that Jesus suffered and died on the cross.

Altar/table

◆ Many churches have a table or altar upon which bread and wine are prepared for the special service of Holy Communion. This service is known by many different names – Mass, Eucharist or The Lord's Supper.

◆ Most churches have special containers for the bread and the wine. Ask your hosts if the children might have a look at them.

Font/place of baptism

◆ This could be a small tabletop font or a large structure often found near the entrance of the church. Baptism marks the entry of new Christians to the Church family.

◆ In some churches there is a large tank instead of a font for the baptism of adults in which people can be completely immersed in water.

Pulpit/reading desk/lectern

◆ The pulpit is the place where sermons are preached.

◆ The lectern, from where the Bible is read, is often shaped like an eagle with outstretched wings.

Checklist for a visit to a church

Before your visit . . .

. . . think about what the aim and focus of your visit will be. Where in your scheme of work does the visit best fit? It may fit at the beginning, or in the middle as an investigative activity, or perhaps at the end to reinforce what the children have been learning about.

You will need to make contact with . . .

. . . the leader of the church you intend to visit, for example the vicar or the minister. If you are making your arrangement by telephone then you will need to send a letter of confirmation. (It's a good idea to telephone immediately prior to your visit.)

The timing of your visit . . .

It may not always be appropriate to visit during an act of worship so be prepared with an alternative date or time.

Find out . . .

. . . if there are parents who attend this place of worship who could help on the visit. Contact the parents by sending a letter home to explain the nature and purpose of your visit. Have a meeting for the parents/helpers who intend to come with you, to brief them about the visit.

Make a preliminary visit to the church . . .

. . . to familiarize yourself with the architecture, features, decorations, people and atmosphere of the place of worship. This will help you to develop preparatory work and the programme for the visit. On a practical note, find out about toilets, wheelchair access and the number of children who can be accommodated.

Tell your hosts about . . .

. . . the age and ability of the pupils, the length of your visit, the focus of the visit and how this relates to work already done, and your proposed programme for the visit.

Ask your hosts about . . .

◆ parts of the church where it is not appropriate for the children to go;

◆ items that should not be touched;

◆ taking photographs, using a flash, using tape recorders or camcorders;

◆ appropriate areas for children to use drawing and writing materials;

◆ whether the building will be empty or whether worshippers will be present during your visit;

◆ whether a small gift would be acceptable as thanks for their hospitality.

Prepare your children . . .

◆ by telling them what will be expected of them;

◆ by familiarizing them with what they are likely to see;

◆ by introducing them to key words they are likely to hear.

On the day of your visit . . .

◆ check that the arrangements are still convenient and that you are expected;

◆ take all the necessary equipment for any activities;

◆ brief a pupil to say 'thank you'.

After your visit . . .

◆ invite your host to visit the school (this could extend the relationship between school and faith community);

◆ send thank you letters and examples of the work that pupils have produced;

◆ extend the visit with activities and reflection upon what the children saw, felt and learnt.

Resources

General

Martin Wallace, *The Celtic Resource Book*, National Society/Church House Publishing, 1998.

Carole Armstrong, *Lives and Legends of the Saints*, Frances Lincoln, 1995.

An attractive collection of paintings by well-known western artists accompanied by stories and information about Christian saints.

Alan Brown and Alison Seaman, *Christian Church*, A & C Black, 1997.

Illustrated text introducing central Christian beliefs and practices on a visit to a church.

Margaret Cooling and Diane Walker with Maggie Goodwin, *Resource Bank Books 1, 2 and 3*, Bible Society, 1993.

Resource books for teaching Bible stories presented through themes.

Ann Druilt, Christine Fynes-Clinton and Marije Rowling, *All Year Round*, Hawthorn Press, no date.

A detailed resource book that explores religious and cultural festivals throughout the seasons.

Kenneth Grahame, *The Wind in the Willows*, 1908, Penguin Books, 1983.

Robert Jackson, Margaret Barratt and Judith Everington, *Bridges to Religions*, Heinemann, 1994.

In particular 'An egg for Babcha' and 'Lucy's Sunday'. This series looks at religious belief and practice through the experiences of children in the faith communities. Teachers' support materials describe the approach and suggest activities.

Graham Owen and Alison Seaman, *Looking at Christianity*, Wayland, 1998.

The 'Looking at Christianity' series includes *Worship, Jesus and Mary, Special Occasions* and *Festivals*. The books are designed for pupils at Key Stage 1.

Janet and John Perkins and Helen Thacker, *Haffertee Hamster*, Lion, 1995.
Pupils' Books and Teacher's Handbook

Christian themes introduced through the adventures of Haffertee Hamster.

Jane Ray, *The Story of the Creation*, Orchard, 1992.

The story of the Creation as found in the first book of the Bible, beautifully illustrated.

Lois Rock, *A First Look Series*, Lion, 1994.

A series of project books with an accompanying Teacher Handbook which explores such things as God, Jesus and the Bible.

David Rose, *Christianity Photopack*, Folens, 1995.

Poster pack with accompanying notes for teachers and suggested activities.

Philip Sauvain, *Famous Lives – Saints*, Wayland, 1996.

The stories of saints retold for young pupils.

Alison Seaman, *My Christian Life*, Wayland, 1996.

An introduction to Christianity for pupils at Key Stage 1. Includes teachers' notes.

Alison Seaman and Alan Brown, *My Christian Faith*, Evans, 1998.

An introduction to Christianity through the experiences of a Christian family. Includes teachers' notes. Also in 'Big Book' format.

David Self, *Stories from the Christian World*, Macdonald, 1998.

Stories about well-known Christians who have by their works and actions tried to express their faith through service to others. Includes Saint Francis and Mother Theresa.

Mary Stone, *Don't Just Do Something, Sit There*, RMEP, 1992.

Activities designed to promote children's spiritual development.

Angela Wood, *Christian Church*, Franklin Watts, 1998.
An introduction to Christian beliefs and practice for pupils at Key Stage 1.

Places of worship (programme 1 *Christianity*), BBC Video, 1997.
A video recording of an infant baptism with accompanying teacher's notes and poster pack.

Christian festivals — general

Nicola Currie, *Festival Allsorts*, The National Society/Church House Publishing, 1994.

Nicola and Stuart Currie, *Seasons and Saints for the Christian Year*, The National Society/Church House Publishing, 1998.
Activities for children with background information for teachers. Covers the Christian year.

Nicola Currie and Jean Thomson, *Seasons, Saints and Sticky Tape*, The National Society/Church House Publishing, 1992.
Activities for children with background information for teachers. Covers the Christian year.

Pam Macnaughton and Hamish Bruce (eds), *Together for Festivals*, The National Society/Church House Publishing, 1997.

Lois Rock, *Festivals of the Christian Year*, Lion, 1996.
Things to make and do at festival times.

Christian festivals — Easter

Pat Alexander, *Song of the Morning*, Lion, 1997.

A. Elwell Hunt, *The Tale of Three Trees*, Lion, 1989.

Freddie the Leaf, video, Educational Media International, 1985.
The story of Easter.

Jan Pienkowski, *Easter*, Heinemann, 1989.
A retelling of the Bible account of Easter.

The Proud Tree, St Paul's Multi Media, no date

Teaching RE: Easter 5-14, Christian Education Movement, 1993.
Background information for teachers with suggested activities.

Helen Thacker, *Haffertee's First Easter*, Lion, 1995.

Brian Wildsmith, *The Easter Story*, Oxford University Press, 1993.
A retelling of the Bible account of Easter.

Christian festivals — Christmas

James Berry, *Celebration Song*, Hamish Hamilton, 1994.
The Christmas story retold in Creole.

Tomie de Paula, *Christmas Story*, Methuen, 1984.

Festival Friezes 1 and 2, poster pack, Pictorial Charts Educational Trust, 1995.
Christmas E752 and E753.

Christina Goodings, *Celebrating Christmas*, Lion, 1998.
Craft, art and stories for Christmas.

Jane Ray, *The Story of Christmas*, Orchard, 1991.

Teaching RE: Christmas 5–14, Christian Education Movement, 1992.
Background information for teachers and ideas for activities.

Julie Vivas, *The Nativity*, Cambridge University Press, 1986.
Traditional words of the Christmas story with unusual illustrations.

Brian Wildsmith, *A Christmas Story*, Oxford University Press, 1989.
Also available as a CD ROM narrated by Martin Jarvis.

Bibles and Bible stories

Animated Bible Stories, video, Channel 4 Learning, 1998.
Stories adapted by Brian Truman based on stories retold by Tim and Jenny Wood.

Bible Stories of the Life of Jesus, CD ROM, Lion.

Sidney Carter and J. Morris, *Lord of the Dance*, Lion, 1998.
Stories of Jesus retold from the Bible.

Tomie de Paola, *The Parables of Jesus*, Lutterworth Press, 1987.

Tomie de Paola, *The Miracles of Jesus*, Lutterworth Press, 1987.

John Drane, *The New Lion Encyclopaedia of the Bible*, Lion, 1998.
A useful picture reference for the historical and geographical setting of biblical events.

Karyn Henley, *The Beginner's Bible*, Kingsway Publications, 1989.
An appropriate Bible for early readers.

My First Bible Stories, CD ROM, Dorling Kindersley, 1997.

Jennifer Rees Larcombe, *Best Bible Stories*, Marshall Pickering, 1996.
Bible stories retold for young children, including 'The man who was not tall enough' (the story of Zacchaeus) and 'The baby in the basket' (the story of Moses).

Stories From the Beginning of Time, CD ROM, Lion, 1997.

The Good News Bible, Bible Society, latest edition, 1994.
A well-respected and 'user friendly' translation of the Bible.

Music

Alleluya, A & C Black, 1981.

Sylvia Barratt and Sheena Hodge, *Tinderbox*, A & C Black, 1982.

P. Burt, P. Horrobin and G. Leavers (compilers), *Junior Praise,* combined music edition, Marshall Pickering, 1997.

Carol, Gaily Carol, A&C Black, 1973.

Peter Churchill, *Feeling Good*, The National Society/Church House Publishing, 1994.

Chris Deshpande and Julia Eccleshare, *Spring Tinderbox*, A & C Black, 1992.

Beatrice Harrop, *Someone's Singing Lord*, A & C Black, 1973.

Judy Jarvis (ed.), *Big Blue Planet*, Stainer and Bell, 1996.

Jump Up if you're Wearing Red, The National Society/Church House Publishing, 1996.

Geoffrey Marshall Taylor, *The Complete Come and Praise*, BBC Books, 1990.

Music From Taizé, Collins Liturgical Press, 1981.

Peter Smith, *New Orbit Songs and Hymns*, Galliard, 1972.

Christian artefacts to collect

◆ rosary beads
◆ cross
◆ palm cross
◆ crucifix
◆ Easter egg
◆ a statue of the mother of Jesus
◆ icons
◆ fish shape
◆ Advent calendar
◆ Advent candle holder
◆ Advent wreath
◆ nativity set
◆ frankincense
◆ myrrh
◆ shell for baptism

Artefacts for the Eucharist

◆ cup (chalice)
◆ plate (paten)
◆ bread
◆ wine
◆ white cloth (corporal)

Candles

◆ Easter
◆ votive
◆ Advent
◆ baptism

Cards

◆ baptism
◆ wedding
◆ confirmation
◆ Easter
◆ Christmas

Certificates

◆ baptism
◆ wedding

Christian Aid, Tear Fund and CAFOD produce a range of audio-visual material that illustrates Christianity in many different cultural settings.

Addresses

Artefacts to Order

Sue Perry

To order Telephone/fax:

01945 587452

Comprehensive collection of religious and cultural artefacts to support the teaching of RE in schools and colleges. Supplied by teachers for teachers.

Articles of Faith

Resource House

Kay Street

Bury

Lancs BL9 6BU

Tel: 0161 763 6232

Religious artefacts for all the major world faiths. Mail order brochure available.

The Children's Society

Edward Rudolf House

Margery Street

London WC1X 0JL

Tel: 0171 837 4299

Produces free support material every year for Christingle services.

Christian Education Movement

Royal Buildings

Victoria Street

DERBY DE3 1GW

Tel: 01332 296655

A comprehensive collection of booklets and posters. Brochure available

Pictorial Charts Educational Trust

PCET, 27 Kirchen Road

London W13 0UD

Tel: 0181 567 9206

A wide variety of pictures, posters and wallcharts. Brochure available.

Religion in Evidence

Unit 7

Monk Road

ALFRETON

Derbyshire DE55 7RL

Tel: 01773 830255

Religious artefacts and posters.

St Paul Multi Media Centre

199 Kensington High Street

London W8 6BA

Tel: 0171 937 9591

Roman Catholic Centre with a wide range of Christian materials for religious education. Branches also in Birmingham, Liverpool and Glasgow.